Praise for

THE FIRST DOMINO

"Tim Castle has done something special with *The First Domino*. This isn't just a book about strategy – it's about what happens when you lead with heart. A powerful reminder that success starts with how you show up for others."

– **Will Guidara, Author of** *Unreasonable Hospitality*

"Most people wait for opportunity. This book teaches you to create it. Read it. Apply it. And watch everything change."

– **James Lawrence, The Iron Cowboy**

"Tim Castle hands you the playbook for creating your own big break, no permission required ... It's the catalyst you've been waiting for."

– **Mark Raffan, Author and Founder of Negotiations Ninja**

"One decision. One action. That's all it takes to change everything. Tim Castle delivers the mindset and method to tip the first domino and never look back."

– **David Meltzer, Chairman of the Napoleon Hill Institute**

AVAILABLE BY THE SAME AUTHOR

The Art of Negotiation:
How to get what you want (every time)

Be The Lion:
How To Overcome Big Challenges And Make It Happen

The Art of Decision Making:
How to make effective decisions under pressure

The Momentum Sales Model:
How to achieve success in sales, exceed targets and generate explosive growth

THE FIRST DOMINO

How to land your first client in 90 days or less

TIM CASTLE

First published in 2025 by Lion House Publishing Ltd.

LION HOUSE
PUBLISHING

US Paperback ISBN: 978-1-0682624-0-1
International Paperback ISBN: 978-1-0682624-1-8
eBook ISBN: 978-1-0682624-2-5

Copyright © 2025 Tim Castle

The moral right of the author has been asserted.

All rights reserved; no part of this publication may be reproduced, stored in a retrieval system, or transmitted in any form or by any means, electronic, mechanical, photocopying, recording, or otherwise without the prior written permission of the Author and Publisher. This book may not be lent, resold, hired out or otherwise disposed of by way of trade in any form of binding or cover other than that in which it is published without the prior written consent of the Author and Publisher.

While every effort has been made to ensure that information in this book is accurate, no liability can be accepted by the Author or Publisher for any loss incurred in any way whatsoever by any person relying on the information contained herein.

No responsibility for loss occasioned to any person or corporate body acting or refraining to act as a result of reading material in this book can be accepted by the Author or Publisher.

The scanning, uploading, and distributing of this book via any means without permission of the Author and Publisher is illegal and punishable by law. No part of this work may be used or reproduced in any manner whatsoever to train or inform artificial intelligence or to teach any computerized system in any way.

Book design by Christopher Parker

www.timjscastle.com

FOREWORD
BY DAVID MELTZER

Entrepreneur | Investor | Speaker | Chairman of the Napoleon Hill Institute

I'VE spent decades building businesses, investing in people, and helping others turn setbacks into stepping stones. And if there's one truth I've learned that *The First Domino* captures beautifully, it's this: **all it takes is one bold move, one committed decision, to create a cascade of success.**

That's what Tim Castle has given you here – a real, practical, momentum-building system rooted in both belief and execution. This book doesn't just talk about business theory. It walks with you through the fire. It gives you the mindset to endure it, the tools to navigate it, and the energy to rise above it.

When I lost everything – and then rebuilt from scratch – it wasn't because of some secret strategy. It was because I learned how to show up with consistency, to stay aligned with my values, and to take purposeful action even when it was hard. That's the spirit of *The First Domino*. It meets you where you are – in the chaos, in the self-doubt, in the moment where quitting feels easier - and it shows you how to *move anyway.*

Whether you're an entrepreneur launching your first offer, a sales professional chasing that breakthrough deal, or a visionary ready to create your own economy, The First Domino will fast-track your journey. It's packed with tools that work — not someday, but **today.**

You'll learn how to reduce friction, take bolder action, trust your gut, and - my favorite - operate with love. Yes, love. Because generosity is a multiplier, and connection is the ultimate currency in business.

Tim gets it. He's walked the walk. This isn't theory. It's lived wisdom - and it's delivered in a voice that fires you up and grounds you in truth.

This is the kind of book I wish I had earlier in my journey. But I'm grateful it exists now, for you - and for the leaders you'll inspire once you knock over your first domino.

So take a deep breath, commit fully, and let this book be the ignition. The moment you stop hesitating. The moment everything changes.

You're only one domino away.

DAVID MELTZER

This is
a book about
magic...

BUT first, let's address the elephant in the room. You are going to die. It's a fact and, depending on where you are at in life on a number of dimensions from health, relationships, stress, genetic predisposition and lifestyle, you've most likely got between ten to fifty summers left on planet earth.

Re-read that last sentence. Let it sink in.

I know it is morbid to think in terms such as these, but by starting here and getting this ingrained in your psyche my hope is it will help you to **prioritise** the right things, get razor-focused on delivering one hundred percent for your business and get serious about continual self-development. The truth is that it is all on you. The good news is that you have the power to change your situation and to increase your awareness of what's possible for you. The decisions you make today have the potential to affect generations of your family to come, but you've got to be fully committed.

> "There is a difference between interest and commitment. When you're interested in something you only do it when it is convenient. When you're committed to something, you accept no excuses, only results."
>
> **– KEN BLANCHARD**

Let's call it out right now, are you all in? All in, in terms of your mind, or are you holding back? Your conscious thoughts shape your reality, and without going too deep, your subconscious reveals the thoughts, plans and ideas you need to make real any suggestion that you give it. So, I'll ask you again, are you all in? Totally committed? Have a quick gut check and be honest with yourself. This is the starting point to your bigger future. You can't have a lukewarm commitment, you must be willing in body, mind and spirit to do whatever it takes on days you don't feel like it. To discipline yourself and take action regardless. Fulfilment is action towards the right goal.

Sentences that start with "If this happens", "I think", "I hope", "I'll give it a try", are all phrases of the interested, not the committed. I need you to take a look at that, your language, the way you are communicating to others and (most importantly) to yourself on a daily basis. I need you to refine it, get it crystal clear, primed for success. I need you fully committed, locked and loaded, so that nothing could deter you, stop you, sway you from doing your best to make this business an outrageous sky-rocketing success.

I want you to walk away from reading this book changed, a new, stronger, more resilient, and faith-filled, inspired you. I want you to take more risks, have richer experiences, see an abundance of good in the world. Critically, I aim to have you prepared for when opportunity strikes, which it will.

The worst thing that could happen is to have a huge opportunity land in your lap and not be ready for it. That's why you must always be developing and honing your sales skills. It is the number one high-leverage skill in the world and you're about to go all the way with it.

From this point on, I want you to remember this conversation. Remember that time is slipping away and that what you do today in this moment has the power to protect, provide for and take care of your family, your children and your children's children. To say it has a big impact is the understatement of the century. I truly hope this realisation makes your hungrier, more committed, and ready to do the work required to make the dream that was put inside of you a reality. The desire you have to see your business flourish was put in you for a reason, you were given this gift for a reason, and now you need to take it to the next level, to rise above it all and execute your vision.

So, this book is about magic. It's about changing your attitude at the exact time you want to give up, and pack it all in. You may even be at that point right now, and that's why you decided to pick up this book. If so, excellent, you are in the right place, but don't you dare throw in the towel, this is when everything is about to change.

You must go from expecting the worst to expecting the best, to being in the finest attitude even when adversity strikes, even when it is hard, and you don't know where your first client is going to come from, even when you don't think you can do it. This is the exact moment that you are ready for a breakthrough, if you just stick with it long enough, consistently enough to reap the rewards. After all, it's exactly when you are about to give up that the transformation occurs.

You have magic within you. How do I know this? Because this dream was hand-selected for you. That fire inside that you feel when I talk about changing your family forever, protecting them for generations to come, and leaving a legacy – that's your truth speaking to you and through you.

Maybe you have a desire to change the world. To create something that radically improves lives, to reimagine how we live today. Whatever your dream is, it is in you for a reason.

You were born to do this, and I applaud you for sticking with it

THE FIRST DOMINO

on the days that everything sucks, when the wind and rain blows in your face, cars drive by and soak you head to toe, you face rejection after rejection, and you just won't quit. That's being fully committed. That's First Domino material.

Now, let's fast track this process so you can create the domino effect and keep getting bigger and bigger wins. Once you master this principle, you'll wonder why you didn't see it before, where it was hiding all this time and what took you so long to find it. However, the reason is, that you will have changed, you will have become more.

The process of doing the challenges and practising the tactics in this book caused you to grow, to develop and expand your awareness. Now you are changed, transformed, and you'll never not know how to do this. To everyone else it will look effortless, like you are manifesting an abundance of sales, or you just keep getting lucky, but throughout this book I am going to pull back the curtain and reveal the secret to making the dominoes fall. The difference is you are willing to do the work, to build leverage into your sales process and to show up consistently. By following these steps, you will become a rainmaker, a game changer and a magician. I guess that makes me a magician trainer; well, it's a title I am happy to bear. This book has been carefully crafted to guide you on the journey.

The one thing I ask is that, if this book helps you, then you should share it with someone else who could use it. This isn't to sell more books, although public reviews are amazing and word of mouth really helps to spread the message, but it's about helping others to become their fullest selves.

A significant portion of this book's profits are going to help children struggling with learning difficulties and people who are less fortunate than ourselves. Some have had their businesses and livelihoods ruined by natural disasters and have no way to provide for their families. It will create a moment of magic in their lives.

THIS IS A BOOK ABOUT MAGIC...

By spreading the word and doing what you can to share this message you are not only adding prosperity to other entrepreneurs, founders and sales professionals, who add immense value to the future of the world, but you are contributing to something on a deeper fundamental level, helping people who've lost everything have the chance to rebuild.

It would mean the world to me if together we could change lives at all levels by spreading the message.

> "To know that even one life has breathed easier because you have lived. This is to have succeeded."
>
> **– RALPH WALDO EMERSON**

The FIRST DOMINO — FREE RESOURCES

- 10 Domino Challenges Chart
- 15 Cold Email Templates
- The First Domino Checklist
- LinkedIn Post Templates
- Big Buckets Tracker and more

Spark a chain reaction of sales success

NOTE TO READER

WHAT you are holding is so much more than just a book. There are several free downloads that will help you to streamline the process of landing your first client, aka, the first domino. These extras accompany the challenges, suggestions and mantras thoughtfully placed throughout this book. Think of them as boosters, they will turbo charge your transformation and help you to get the most out of the journey you are about to embark on.

There's a downloadable *The First Domino* workbook too. This will allow you to gain clarity and stay in control, reducing your stress levels to the point where this process becomes fluid, effortless and easy.

Using this material in conjunction with these extras is the most effective way to see the dominoes fall in a repeatable fashion so you can gain momentum for your business. By working through each challenge, not only will you experience a meteoric rise towards mastery, but you'll visualise your progress along the way, which will help you to stay committed throughout.

Hop on over to **www.thefirstdominobook.com** to download your free workbook now.

CONTENTS

THE STARTING POINT   1

THE FIRST DOMINO FRAMEWORK   9

CHAPTER 1
Reduce the friction   11

CHAPTER 2
Do impossible things   35

CHAPTER 3
Trust your intuition   53

CHAPTER 4
Be a magic maker   69

CHAPTER 5
Get an epic life   97

CHAPTER 6
Question everything   115

CHAPTER 7
Adopt the mindset   139

CHAPTER 8
Remember love											157

CHAPTER 9
Tell the story											167

CHAPTER 10
Become a magnet										179

CHAPTER 11
Create your economy									193

CHAPTER 12
Securing your first domino							205

## SOURCES											238

## BOOKS THAT INSPIRED ME							239

THE STARTING POINT

NEVER let life beat you down. We all face times when we're in the storm, when we have a week that kicks our ass, and we want to throw in the towel.

We question ourselves. Do I really have what it takes? Why hasn't it happened yet? Am I good enough?

I understand it may feel like the world is against you right now and everyone's watching. You might be facing a series of client rejections, people that were supposed to be for you are showing their true colours and not supporting you, life is coming at you, and you are toying with the idea of giving up.

When this happens, you have a choice to make. These crossroads will come up every now and again. It's just part of the journey and it's where you make the most important decision.

When this happens, you can choose to treat yourself with compassion and respect. To never let the external situation undermine your value. The thing to note is that your value never changes, despite what accolades you achieve, what wins you rack up and what other people say. When we are winning and things are going our way, it can be easy to think that we are worthy of it and that we have value.

However, when the tide goes out, that's when we need to retain that same mindset. Instead, we often let our external circumstances dictate how we feel and how we see ourselves when it comes to value. This is where we must take a strong view, remembering that, regardless of the applause or silence, our value doesn't change.

This can be especially hard when we change from one job to the next, where we might have built up a reputation, won sales awards, proven ourselves already and now we enter a new culture, a potentially hostile environment, where our results have yet to be delivered. It can lead you to believe that, unless you deliver big results in record time, you aren't worth the same as before. This is where we must take ultimate control because nothing controls your value except you. You get to choose how you see you. I want you to always see your full worth and appreciate it, regardless of what's going on around you.

I'll share you a brilliant story to drive this home.

A professor stood in front of his class, held up a crisp $100 bill and asked, "How much is this worth?"

"$100," the class replied in unison.

The professor then crumpled the bill into a ball and held it out in his palm and asked. "How much is this worth now?"

"$100," the students replied.

The professor threw the bill on the ground, stomped on it and asked, "And how about now?"

Looking confused at their professor's actions, the students shrugged and answered, "$100."

The professor smiled and said, "Good! Remember this lesson in your own life. Whatever happens, however people treat you, whatever circumstances befall you, your value remains the same."

This story is an important lesson: always choose to see your full value.

Other people and situations don't control your value, whether you get crumpled, stomped on or chucked away, your value is the constant.

Don't let your self-worth get tied to winning awards, your past successes, things people said about you ten years ago, your bank balance, your stock portfolio, press releases, the court of public opinion, your current sales figures, pipeline or anything else external. This journey is an inside-out job.

Choose to appreciate you, just as you are, for your full value, and your full worth.

This way you will stay in control. As a sales professional ready to up their game or a CEO and Founder of a startup burning through capital, energy and their sanity on the hunt for their first client, I know you might be feeling overwhelmed and stressed, questioning why it is so damn hard to get what you want. I understand that you've got to make it work, that people are depending on you to pull this off, that it matters. Not only investors, but your friends and family, your hopes and dreams are in this bet. Whether you've just started a new job in sales and need to deliver results and revenue impact or you're a Founder or leader of a business and everything is on the line. I know how it feels to have the pressure of building a business that needs to work. I know how badly you want that first client to come in, so that you can show the world just how awesome your business is and that you can get to the next stage, all whilst providing a decent lifestyle for your family and feeling like you are making progress, delivering value and winning.

The first step, aside from always choosing to appreciate your full value, is to put some things in place that will allow you to feel more in control, to stop the emotional ups and downs and the feeling of overwhelm.

My first recommendation is that you should put in place the big rocks tracker and then never deviate from it. It's available as a free template for you at **www.thefirstdominobook.com**. I want you to succeed so I am sharing the most valuable tools with you upfront so you can hit the ground running.

You will find that this first step is an invaluable one! It will help you to streamline your daily actions so that you can focus on producing high quality weeks consistently. It will also help you see how far you have come. It's simple to complete, just fill out each big rock, you want to have 5-6 of these. A big rock is an area you are solidly focused on that will help your business grow. For example, this could be prospecting and planting seeds, marketing and events, nurturing clients, networking, pipeline development.

Fill out your big rocks so that you can tackle and prioritise them every day. With this new level of direction towards your goal achieving activities, the biggest needle-movers for the metrics you care about – in this case, landing your first flagship client. It will have an outsized impact on your business growth. There are certain behaviours and actions that will increase the likelihood of success. Maintaining a consistent and deliberate bias towards action around these big rocks is where you elevate.

The next column is for your deliverables and actions (what you have done). After that, the final column is for comments, so that you can capture any vital notes you don't want to forget (e.g. the things you think you'll remember but ultimately forget).

I recommend that the first time you complete this exercise

should be on a walk or somewhere quiet. You can get out a fresh piece of paper and brainstorm, noting down your top priority big rocks. You want to be crystal clear when identifying and targeting the biggest needle-moving areas of focus for your specific business.

The importance of this document cannot be overstated. Once you have everything out on the page and it is tracked weekly, you will feel more in control. Action is always the way out of anxiety, out of doubt and into confidence. Action is what makes the difference. Too many folk plan to plan, get stuck in a constant loop of thought and never take any significant action. Take action and recognise that you have the magic inside to create the vision and bring it to life. Follow that thought process.

This document will transform your business and your sales process into a lean, focused arrow that flies directly into the target. It will also provide you with a reference point so you can see all the inspired big actions you have taken, over the course of each week. As this builds up, nothing will be able to mess with your state of inner calm because everything you need to do is documented, captured and available.

As a result, you will feel more in control. If you're a salesperson, share this with your manager and get their buy-in. It demonstrates proactiveness, reliability and that you've got it under control.

Now, I will offer a final word on your mindset before we get started (sidenote – it's always funny when an author does this and builds up the anticipation, when in reality we have already started, and the transformation is already underway. All it takes is one sentence said in the right way with the right fire behind it for it to land and set you on course for massive success). So, here is a final word, or thought, before we jump in: stand guard to what you let in your mind. In fact, be overly aware.

Here are a couple of quick tweaks I want you to implement right away: 1) quit watching the news from now on; it's just filled with pessimistic, doom-ridden angst that you don't need in your content diet; and 2) reduce your proximity to perpetual complainers. This means not letting other people's "negative suggestions" anywhere near you. Your mind is like a speaker, it soaks up and amplifies whatever you give it. You think on a frequency, so we want to make sure you are unceasingly tuned in to Good Vibes FM.

Take stock of how you have been thinking lately. Be very careful what you think and say; from now on, if you catch yourself thinking or verbalising ideas that aren't fully committed, or stem from the seeds of fear, doubt and worry, immediately counteract this with its opposite. We need to get your mind reprogrammed and back on track to a world of plentiful abundance.

Think and speak about the amazing things that are happening, how success is raining down on you, and expect your vision to come to life. Start programming yourself to see the good that is all around you and boost your faith that it will all happen for you. When someone asks you how you are, you say "fantastic", "on fire", "loving life", "incredible", "outstanding", and "I'm truly grateful". These are all first domino approved responses you can adopt. By doing this you are signaling to your unconscious mind the world you want to see. Thoughts are things. It's a subtle but meaningful shift, and it has an outsized impact on your results.

Stop saying "I'm not bad", "I'm alright", "I'm surviving", as if that's acceptable. It's not. Far from it, in fact.

How can you expect to have a miraculously awe-inspiring life if every day you are feeding your mind with worry, speaking fear and anxiety into your plans and telling the world you are "not bad", as if that's somehow a good thing! It's mediocre and poverty minded. Rid these statements from your life from this moment onwards and don't look back, no matter what is happening in the external world. Start now and program yourself in every area of your life to see the good you desire, in health, finances, relationships, and business, every negative thought must be counteracted with its positive equivalent.

> "Think good, and good follows. Think evil, and evil follows. You are what you think all day long."
>
> **– JOSEPH MURPHY**

THE FIRST DOMINO FRAMEWORK

As I alluded to at the very beginning, this book is about magic, and magic stands for something more in this context. These are the steps to guide your every interaction, to show emotional intelligence in sales and to activate the first domino.

The first domino has a framework. Throughout this book, I want you to keep this handy framework in mind to ensure that you are on track to sales success. You will see tenants of this philosophy scattered throughout, with the aim of accelerating your sales and business expansion. This is MAGIC.

M ake connections everywhere you go
A dd value
G ive willingly
I nspire others' growth
C ollaborate

If you hold these values as true, you can't fail to win. Your sales process – guided by these core attributes – becomes leveraged and leads to the impression of growth in every interaction allowing you to unlock new realms of possibility.

Make connections everywhere you go	Pour into others and breathe life into your dreams.
Add value	By making valuable introductions, referrals, and recommendations.
Give willingly	Without expectation of something in return, although you know that it's all working in your favour.
Inspire others' growth	Through your own shining example and encouragement.
Collaborate	For this is the real magic.

I don't want to labour the point by going into any more detail than this. The purpose of this book is to give you tactics and strategies to embody the framework as you go about your sales conversations and interactions. It's about who you become, not what you understand but don't act upon.

CHAPTER 1
REDUCE THE FRICTION

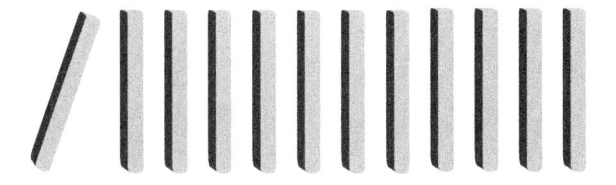

1. PROSPECTING

Let's start with how to master the cold email.
The first step is to become unattached. Neutral. The more attached you are, the more it owns you. Cold emails tend to stress out the inexperienced business development (BD) person; because they fear being rejected, they don't have any strategies to deploy if no one responds and, because they haven't had enough failed attempts, they don't know how to come back – to play the game – and this fuels this anxiety-ridden mindset. That's why, if this resonates with you, we're going to start with your mindset. If you're an experienced deal hunter, this is also for you; we all need a reminder every now and again to stay neutral, detached, and cool.

The mindset you want to employ is that the cold email is all about planting seeds. The email is your first shot across the bow; it's a broad open collaborative "hey there, we've got something of value, and I reckon you might be interested". The cold email needs a hook, one singular point of focus, a why. This can be related to a topic, an idea, and the point is to motivate action, but this has to come from you.

Based on your business, you can approach this from the perspective of "we're doing X and we help clients with Y. Here's a few results." Don't overthink it. You want to know the secret? The more well-constructed and tailored cold emails you send, the more in tune you'll get to what resonates. It can be a word change, a different way of phrasing things, but trust me, there is a way to

THE FIRST DOMINO

present the information in a few (3-5) sentences that will provoke the intrigue and the action you want. It's not rocket science, but it does take practice.

The mistake both rookies and experienced salespeople make is that they allow themselves to sound cheesy. They push their own product way too much and don't make their emails resonate with that specific individual.

If you're facing the deafening sound of no responses to the 15 emails you sent today, I hate to break it to you, but you need to do more; you need to refine your work, to get in tune, to feel the energy as you write these emails. It's consistency not intensity that wins. 15 a day and you'll improve. You are practising your craft and, as the entrepreneur in your business, you have to wear all the hats. The excuse that you haven't done it before, or it's not working, doesn't cut it. It's you, not them. Your email composition needs more care, so take the time to read your email. Would you respond to it? How's your mindset towards cold emails? Do you see them as planting seeds or would you rather be doing something else, like coding?

Have you ever listened to the song *Adventure of a Lifetime* by Coldplay? If not, turn it on right now. It's a magical feeling. It feels like things can happen, right? Doors can open. Once you get the cold email down and you get a response, then you are going to feel on top of the world. You'll be flying so high you'll probably do a little jump for joy… but not so fast, Sally! I don't want to burst your bubble, but this is the exact moment you should use this feeling to blast out 20 more cold emails. Celebrate for a second, do a jump and fist pump the air before going right back to your inbox and working it.

Be sure to check out the email you sent that got a reply. How was it composed? How were you feeling when you wrote it? Were you relaxed, unattached to the outcome? Now copy and paste that email structure to a new message and use your excitement to write

CHAPTER 1: REDUCE THE FRICTION

for the next 30 minutes at least. I want to see you use this vitality, this energy, to plant more seeds. When is the best time to make a sale? Right after you just made a sale! It's the same with cold emails. Send them out, Sally. Think of your cold emails as being door openers – that's all they are. No biggy. No need to sell everything in one shot. No need to ram everything you know about their industry down their throat. No need to overshare or oversell. These are the mistakes made by rookies; they blow their load on the cold email and have nothing left in the tank for a meeting. However, they need not worry because, when you behave like this, there will be no meeting, no progression, no magic.

Now you are thinking of your cold emails as door openers, the goal is to get the meeting. This should give you an idea of how to declutter your current cold email, allowing it to shine whilst also keeping it real and doing it justice. After all, it's your first impression, and that means you want to keep a bit of mystery. This is how you use the psychology of human behaviour to your advantage, creating intrigue and, you guessed it, creating value.

Rookies share everything in the first email because they fear that, if it's not in there, they won't hook the client... or maybe that they'll miss the opportunity. But this fear is costing them big time because there's nothing to get curious about and their email is a turn off. Your job is knowing what to cut and what to keep in. It's all about strategy. This is the skill and it is developed through practice. You'd be surprised what works. Less can be more in this instance. Standing out can be better than sounding like a robot powered by Chat GPT trying to mask the fear of a 40-year-old executive that now needs to land a client, and might I add, not just any client, their first client.

Don't underestimate the detrimental effect your situation is having on your ability to send cold emails that trigger a response. I get it. You have a lot riding on this: you've remortgaged the house, taken loans from family and friends, maybe you've raised some seed funding and now you've got to deliver. All eyes are on you, except they're not the right eyes, these are the eyes of people looking to see if you're going to pull it off. I hear you, brother. I hear you, sister. I know why you picked up this book. I know you've got to make it happen. I know what this means to you.

Fear not. We'll get you to be the cold email sensei that you know you can be. But now I am going to need you to put in the reps, to blow off the cobwebs and get your game back. Or maybe even create some game.

Now go to Spotify and play *Baby* by Bakermat. Get it pumping. Doesn't that feel good? Can you feel the love? The possibility. This is the attitude and the vibe I want you to be in when you are writing cold emails. There can be no fear, no desperation, just pure elation – a higher vibration, a new standard.

> Hi Jackie,
>
> I hope you're well.
>
> I wanted to get in touch as I'm now at Planet Race, whose mission is to beat Elon Musk by sending people to Mars first. As part of this, we're helping clients get satellites into orbit on the way there. This means that we have the ability to halve the cost of ordinary satellite launches.
>
> It would be great to explore how we can help Satellites R Us with their payloads and show you the platform. Would you have some time for a call this Friday, or next week sometime?
>
> I've attached a one-pager with more information.
>
> Best,
>
> Tim

Now, I know what you are thinking: Tim, it's too simple! If I don't go into all the detail and tell them about X capability, then I'll miss the opportunity. Or how is this different to what I am writing? But trust me, you've got some fluff in your email that doesn't need to be there. It's weighing you down, so cut it loose, unburden yourself.

RULES FOR SOLID GOLD COLD EMAILS

- Cut the jargon.

- Cut the waffle.

- Cut the weird speak; talk like yourself.

- Greet people how you would actually speak to someone, not like some trumped up knob jock who swallowed a thesaurus and is over complicating the request. Your job with this cold email is firstly to get it opened (use an attractive headline, something personalised to them) and secondly, to get the meeting. That's it!

- Be polite. I see this time and time again from senior sales professionals: skipping the politeness step is a big mistake.

- Don't make demands (e.g. here's my calendar, you can put in a meeting that works for you) – it's way too assumptive.

- Don't suck up.

- Stop trying to sell your product in the first email, this can all come later.

- Talk about the outcome they want; what you can do for them.

You only need this cold email to get you a meeting with them. It doesn't need to do all the work.

Let's assume you send a hundred solid cold emails this week. I mean, pure gold, high-calibre emails with a trigger that promotes action. Let's assume that you have a 10% success rate in landing a meeting from your emails. Congratulations! Well done! This is now the metric to focus on. Double down on what works, try to spot themes between the emails that are getting you meetings.

Take time to reflect on how you felt when you were writing the successful email, the one that got a response and secured a meeting, how did you phrase things? How casual was it? How naturally did it flow? What was the structure of the email? How unattached to the outcome were you? Who were you sending these emails to? What roles were they in? What resonated? What time of day was it? How long did it take for them to respond? Identify what is working and replicate it. Track your success rate of landing a meeting. It tells you something. Cold emails are also about your self image, but more on that later. When you are with the client, ask them what stood out, why they showed an interest. This is all fantastic data to feed the next iteration.

The magic formula is something like this.

- **Personalised Email Header** – stand out and connect instantly. E.g. "The Art of Negotiation – Exclusive Rights Deal – Turkey" or "Their Company x Your Company – Conversion Rates – location" or "Their Company x Your Company – outcome – result."
- **Explain what it is about up front** – "It would be great to catch up regarding…"
- **Must have a hook** that applies specifically to them. "We help (clients like you, give some examples, e.g. Adidas, Nike, Puma) do X and achieve Y (insert outcome and

benefits – e.g. cost saving, make more money, save time, achieve status, reducing risk)."
- **Ask for the meeting.** "Would you be free (here) or (here)?"

Differentiate by being yourself and using normal language attached to what you can help the individual get that they care about. This email will form the bridge from where they are (current reality) to where they want to go (future reality). Your ideas hit home when you nail this message in a couple of sentences. Your business is the bridge between these two worlds.

Do your research, scan their LinkedIn page – what does this person care about? What are they sharing articles on? How long have they been in their current role? If you sense this person is all about getting a promotion, link how what you are doing is helping others with that. If you know they are all about earning more money, driving more revenue, increasing their own status, link it to that – in one short sentence.

The goal is to quickly get to the point by making it clear what you want (the chance to catch up) whilst alluding to how it helps them personally – "Are you still at Union Bank? It would be fantastic to chat more about how we are helping banks to secure more high net worth clients. Would you have some availability next week?"

Here's an example of a Follow-Up email that would almost work but still sounds too robotic and scripted. You've got to loosen up. Put some of yourself in the equation.

Entrepreneurs and top salespeople take one hundred percent ownership of everything they do. I'm glad you're curious and want to learn more; you should be curious as hell, so lean into that muscle, cultivate it on all fronts, ask a lot of questions, become a student of your craft. Right now, that craft is cold emails.

Subject: Follow-up

Hi (First Name),

Quick follow-up question: What does data management (insert the things you do) look like at HSBC (insert their company name)?

Want to move from manual and time consuming (insert pain point) to automated and stress free (insert new world vision and solution)?

Rapid Data (insert your company name) can help you to achieve this and more. Our data management platform (insert platform, data, tech, service) is designed to:

- Add how it reduces risk of xxxx
- Improve xxxx
- Add efficiencies xxxx
- Save costs xxxx
- Make it easy by xxxx

Click here to see the positive impact we've made to companies similar to yours.

Regards,

Tim

You might be thinking, well that sounds pretty good, what's up with that email? But it's the little things that matter, so why does this follow-up email not quite make the cut?

Besides the email header not being inspiring ("Follow-up" is super boring and doesn't scream *read me now, I have something amazing to share with you*) and the signature being in a smaller font to the body of the text, a clear indication that you copied and pasted it from an email template. Which everyone knows comes across as zero fucks given. The main issue is it sounds like R2D2 from *Star Wars* wrote it. It's stale, it has no life and doesn't create impact. It's like you're offering a piece of old bread which has been discarded and is bland, saying "here, do you want this to munch on?" No one wants this, no matter how hungry or in need of your services they

CHAPTER 1: REDUCE THE FRICTION

are. Functionally it's still bread, but it's lost the freshness, vitality and nourishment it needs to stand out. Remember you are a magician, here to inspire wonder, awe and possibility, not put people to sleep with your cookie cutter approach.

Subconsciously, the reader knows you don't really care about them and that's proven by the number of small inconsistencies that add up through the course of those ten sentences.

The standard is high for cold emails and if you want to make the cut you've got to do better. This email lacks personality, spirit and heart. It also sounds generic, like an ad, because that's how it is structured. But you want to know the bigger reason why this type of email fails to cut through even though it looks elegant? It's because everyone is using it, spamming it on LinkedIn, so that now your prospect is psychologically primed to ignore it and not give it the attention it deserves. Also, because it sounds like a template, it sets off alarm bells in the prospect's head that this is just an email you blast out at high volume to try to get a live one. You've got to inject some human into your cold emails, infuse it with your voice and personality, bring it to life.

Here's a better way to bring that out whilst getting your point across.

Subject: Meeting next week?

Hi Sam,

Just following up on the below to see when you'd have availability to meet? We're doing some big things with X, Y and Z clients in the same space and think that there could be some good opportunities to collaborate.

I've attached a case study for your reference.

If you'd be open to explore next week it would be great to find a time to get you across it. Just let me know a time and day that works.

Best,

Tim

When you email as yourself, then you automatically differentiate yourself from everyone else sending crappy automated messages, sucking up with words that make no sense ("I'd LOVE to catch up" in all caps, or "super excited to meet you"). Stop doing this; you are doing yourself an injustice. You have value to offer, except when you pen emails like this and allow yourself to sound like a fan rather than an expert.

There are so many templated or AI-written emails flying around, emails that you literally look at and ask: what are you saying? They use too many complicated words and are filled with nothing real, only hot air and a lax carelessness.

Going back to the R2D2-sounding Follow-Up email, it begins with two questions. The strategy here is to have your prospect imagine their current and ideal situation within the context of what you are selling, but let's get real: when you go with the two-question strategy to get the prospect thinking about how they currently do something and then to how you fix it, what are you risking here?

Think about it: how do you react when you receive this type of email? People are time poor; distractions are heavy and constant. Getting a prospect to actually do the type of thought-provoking imagining you are asking for is rare – it is asking too much. Light bulb moments happen in the shower not at the desk. Time is your prospect's most valuable commodity, so get to the point. Build trust through differentiating how you come across, not just by focusing on what you do for them in relation to what they care about.

The real reason for your follow-up is to secure the first meeting. This should be your primary question. When can we make it happen? The bullet points are overkill, and they make it come across as a pitch rather than an invite to explore something further together. The risk is, if you get these bullet points wrong, they can do more harm than good. Wrong can also mean what

CHAPTER 1: REDUCE THE FRICTION

your prospect interprets them as being and not what you actually meant. The only sentence that actually works is the hook ("click here to see how we've impacted other clients"), which is something you can add into any email you write.

Follow up on every request, absolutely, but make securing a meeting your primary goal. One simple, easy request per email. Make it enjoyable to work with you, and reduce the friction at every interaction. Slowly, you are drip feeding them information about how you work, what you can do for them and where the value is.

Timing also matters. A recent study by Neil Patel conducted analysis of a staggering 1.46 billion emails sent over one year, and here's what they found.

The results were conclusive: the best days to send emails where you want to trigger action are Tuesday, Wednesday and Thursday, and the ideal time is between 9am-12pm. This means you should consider sending your most important emails during these times.

Armed with these insights, this changes everything by using data to inform your prospecting strategy and client engagement; if you want to increase the chances of securing a client meeting, you need to make it easy for them. Reduce the friction, once again. Email them when they are paying attention and itching to reply. Get into their inbox ahead of the pack and stay there. This is when these movers and shakers have a moment free to take action and do things like replying, scheduling a meeting or signing an agreement, so this is the time to do it.

Get scientific about it. Make these times your golden hours for your most crucial impact-driven emails.

Email Marketing Insights
Best Time To Send Emails

Day Of The Week	12 AM to 3 AM	3 AM to 6 AM	6 AM to 9 AM	9 AM to 12 PM	12 PM to 3 PM	3 PM to 6 PM	6 PM to 9 PM	9 PM to 12 PM
Monday	1	1	3	4	3	2	1	1
Tuesday	1	2	3	4	4	4	1	1
Wednesday	1	2	3	4	4	4	1	1
Thursday	1	2	3	5	4	4	2	1
Friday	1	2	3	4	3	2	1	1
Saturday	1	1	2	3	3	2	1	1
Sunday	1	1	3	3	3	2	2	1

Score 1–5

WHAT TO DO NEXT: Consider sending your most important emails from **Tuesday** to **Thursday** between **9am** and **12pm**.

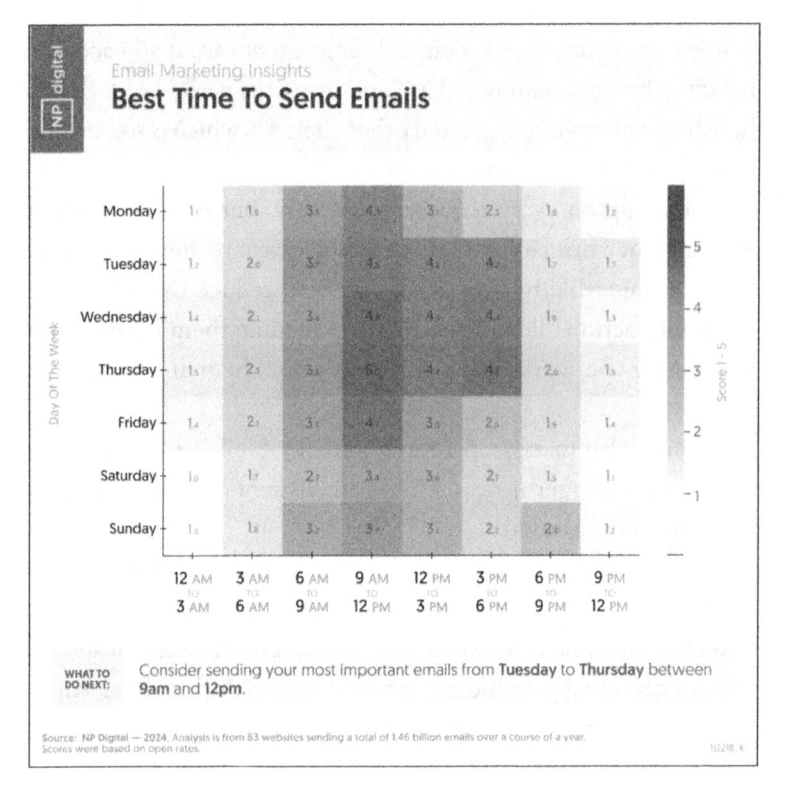

Source: NP Digital — 2024. Analysis is from 83 websites sending a total of 1.46 billion emails over a course of a year. Scores were based on open rates.

Neil Patel, Email Marketing Insights

As I outlined in my book *The Momentum Sales Model*, the 9 before 9am strategy is effective because it hits the client's inbox right as they are sitting down to get into action. When you are planting seeds with 9 potential clients every morning before 9am, you can't help but win big. Rather than scroll to the bottom of all the unread emails, your email floats in at the top and gets automatic attention, which results in quick action.

You are fighting for attention. Of course, this strategy was just an observation I had made when generating momentum to expand tech businesses; 9 before 9am works. Now, with this data

CHAPTER 1: REDUCE THE FRICTION

in hand, I can see how this is an even more targeted approach, allowing you to get maximum effectiveness.

Imagine for a minute that the prospect responds to your follow-up. You've got the first meeting locked in, so let's go through how you should approach this.

2. THE FIRST MEETING

TRY not to wet yourself. Hold yourself back. I can feel your jubilation, but you need restraint. This meeting is for you to uncover and explore. It's not for you to ram everything you've got down their throat. How can you know what they need? It's too presumptive. This meeting helps to inform the next one, but if you come in all ambitious – "Here's what we've got... Do you want it?" – there will be no next meeting.

Do you know what makes you come across more relaxed in meetings? Being less attached to the outcome. That's achieved by having lots of other meetings in the diary. A busy and productive person values their time immensely. A busy person has shit going on. They are a game changer. They've got dominoes falling all over the place and they expect great things to happen. This type of person is magnetic; they live their life as if what they want has already happened. It's this level of certainty that what they want is on the way that guides them towards opportunities and possibilities with ease.

In the eyes of the client, you will be more attractive to them if you are busy, if you've got things going on. Therefore, if you haven't got many clients right now and you're staring at an empty calendar, we need to tune your mindset into becoming someone who has got things going on. This is going to help you to control the neediness and desperation. That urge to show them everything, and worst of all, tell them everything, which ends up in you giving them things for free or conceding things needlessly. Again, this only lowers your value in the eyes of the client.

We need you to be perceived as valuable. Let me be clear: I am not saying you aren't valuable already or valuable as a human being. What I am getting at is how you can use human psychology to your advantage. If you were someone with a business that is on fire – I mean, it's coming in and everyone wants what you've got – how confident would you be? How at ease would you be? How much more valuable would your time be? Your need to land your first client is holding you back from landing your first client. That elusive first domino has to topple.

Therefore, you need to act as the CEO, business executive, BD extraordinaire who's got clients all over the place. You need to be someone who's got things happening, a pipeline filled with clients and exciting deals already in motion.

You need to act as the future version of you would act if these things were real now. The key is in your mind. Visualise this. Go there regularly. See yourself busy, effective and productive. See yourself effortlessly closing deals and shaking hands. Feel the ease and effortlessness with which extraordinary things happen to you and for you. Train yourself to expect great things and tap into the miraculous nature of life. There's a flow of opportunities that is constantly available to you, so get into a relaxed state, clear your mind and use your imagination to produce this reality. This is where all breakthroughs take place and, when they do, make sure you immediately take action in the present. Developing this bias towards action will serve you well, especially when combined with a regular practice of meditation on your bigger future. Often entrepreneurs and salespeople miss out on golden opportunities because they let hesitation, doubt and the age old "I'll do it later" take precedence.

Do you remember that mindset from the start of the chapter?

CHAPTER 1: REDUCE THE FRICTION

You haven't lost anything by securing this meeting; it can only take you closer to getting a deal. The mistake people make is that they come at it from the angle of "What if I don't get the deal?", as if they have something to lose. You must always focus on what you have to gain, coming from a place of abundance instead of lack.

Right now, by having this meeting, you can only increase your chances of progressing the conversation and doing business together. Focus goes where energy flows. Therefore, focus on what you want and see this meeting as a step in the right direction. The only possibility is increase, expansion, and partnership, expect this to happen. The opportunity is right in front of you; when you attend the meeting, focus on uncovering details about their business, objectives and priorities whilst showing patience and restraint. Most people are listening to respond, not listening to understand. Don't be most people. Use the moment to probe with curiosity. You are there to serve.

The goal is to find the pain point that you can solve and build a relationship by showing you care. You are there to qualify how big this pain point is relative to what you do and how well placed you are to solve it. You're there to plant the seed.

The mistake entrepreneurs and salespeople make at this point is that they become too defensive and wedded to their solution. Objections become challenges and, instead of listening, empathising and carefully and calmly walking them through what you are all about, they go all in on proving that the objection is invalid. You're here to plant the seed, but instead, you blow up the whole damn garden and then wonder why you don't get a follow-up.

It's easily done, especially when you are technically minded, passionate and can see the error in another person's thinking. You figure, if I can just fix their thinking, win them over with logic and words, it will solve the problem and they'll have to agree. Instead, this just aggravates the potential customer, and they walk away with the mindset of "I'll think twice about doing business with *that* guy". If this comes up, view the objection as a chance to uncover more about why they think this way, this will help you more than trying to persuade them they are wrong through facts and figures. Spending too much time disproving their objections is the surest way to slow the whole process down; you are responsible for ensuring this does not happen to you.

What you should do instead is a simple sentence, light, easy, frictionless. For example, if they say something like, "I don't think there's much of a market for what you are doing here" then you say, "Can I ask, what makes you think that?" This makes them investigate their own thinking. Remember, you don't need to be convinced that what they are saying is untrue. Once they tell you what assumptions they are making, revealing the data points or references they are using to come to that conclusion, you say (in a light, relaxed tone) "You'd think that. I thought that too, initially. However, big clients like A, B and C are really leaning in". It's less than 15 words and it transitions the conversation away from conflict and into information sharing. In one subtle move you transition from potential adversary to valuable asset and expert. The way you hold yourself during this exchange is everything.

That's the point where you stop; you don't oversell, and you don't go out of your way to prove what you just said. You just follow up with some one-pagers and a creds deck on email after the meeting and then you leave.

As Tywin Lannister said in *Game of Thrones*, "Any man who must say 'I am the king' is no true king."

Let curiosity do its magic: they will ask another question, possibly about pricing, and you can then send through the pricing and wait. Let that seed germinate, let the nutrients do their work. Remember that you are a busy, valuable, interesting and

CHAPTER 1: REDUCE THE FRICTION

productive human. You've got things going on; you're not waiting around watching seeds grow – you're out planting more.

It's this very psychology that will encourage the customer to lean into you. You aren't attached to the outcome, therefore it's free to happen, because you're not needy or restrictive, desperate or lacking in any way.

When we are lacking and opting into this feeling of wanting, we are coming from a place of fear. It's easy as entrepreneurs to be fuelled by dark energy. What if this doesn't happen? What if I can't sign that client? What if I look stupid and lose all my money in front of my friends and family? But it's this very thinking that will cause you to make poor decisions, especially when trying to secure that first flagship client. Don't do this, friend. It's you versus you here!

Fear will lead you to give away too much, overstretch, overanalyse, and undercharge. It will cause you to cling to the idea of who your first client will be and how it should go. Instead of letting it happen and evolve, you force it.

Force is never the way. Deals should flow like water, although that's not to say it won't take massive amounts of grit. You should persist like a river flowing down a mountain, starting off small but finding a way forward. Persist in planting seeds for the future, in creating outsized opportunities, in opening up to possibility – but never try to tie down that one customer because you need it so desperately. Stop trying to force and start learning to attract.

We attract on the creative plane, using our imagination, and living and *feeling* as if the goal has already been achieved. Most entrepreneurs mess up this process, they do all of the goal setting, vision planning and mood boards but then fail to activate one crucial step: they don't cultivate the feeling of their vision being already in existence. Sadly, this leads to them living in a state of wanting; they obsess about *how* it will happen and try to control it. All of this effort is futile. Instead, they should allow themselves the sensation of feeling as if they already had their first client. This is where the river flows fastest, and where ideas and opportunities are like stars in the sky: plentiful.

Your imagination is one of the most powerful forces you possess, but most fail to use it well. It's a topic I feel passionately about and one that, if you get it right, will radically change the whole game. I teach all my students this because, once it clicks, the blockage is removed and the synchronicities, possibilities and results shift into new levels of success.

Ok, so back to your client and the sales process.

Make it easy for them to say "yes", to want to continue, to sell the idea, to make connections that help you in the future. This is all about removing the friction and helping your clients to win and, as a result, landing your first flagship client.

After the meeting is done, it's back down to what you do best: prospecting. Get into the habit of using your moments between meetings to prospect. It's a rhythm. This keeps you on the go, in motion. It helps you to reinforce that image as someone who has got things to do, places to be and a dream to make happen.

One of the most under-utilised areas of business building is the follow-up, so let's double-click on that for a second.

A simple email flow goes something like this:

- Cold email – keep it broad, open, and easy for them to say yes to a meeting.
- Follow-up email – a short jolt that inspires action, a reminder. Primary focus is to get a meeting locked in.
- Follow-up email with a twist – so you stand out, add value and insight or a referral or name drop.
- Follow up with fresh case study – the proof point to influence and nudge.
- Follow up with out of the box thinking – that's when you really nail their need.

CHAPTER 1: REDUCE THE FRICTION

It's not rocket science, but there is an art and a science to it. Far too many entrepreneurs and salespeople let the opportunity slip through the net because they don't know how to inspire action. They overcrowd their emails with information, hoping to snag a point of interest, instead of being clear, authentic and coming from a place of adding value. Oh my goodness, this last one is the truth! Stop filling your email with every single thing you could possibly say: it's OVERWHELMING! It's too much to take in. Just be cool.

Take some time to reflect before you hit send: does your email sound like it comes from someone who values their time, what they have to offer and is an expert in their field?

Or does it sound needy? Does it feel like you are desperate for the meeting so that you can sell them something, even though you don't know whether they need it yet? Did it flow out of you effortlessly or was it punishing to write? Did you overstress, analysing every word?

My general approach is to plant more seeds than I think I'll need. That way, I'll have a bigger crop in the summer, and it also helps to quash any tendency to oversell to the few. The other thing is that, once the dominoes start to fall, there will come a moment that you are tempted to stop the behaviours that got you your first client. This is a mistake. The overconfidence that comes from winning, the feeling that business will always be like this, lulls you into a false sense of security that, if not checked regularly, will be a painful reminder that you messed up.

Don't get rocked to sleep by your success. Never stop planting seeds everywhere you go. However, it always has to be meaningful; keep focused on targeting clients you'd be excited to work with. There's nothing worse than spending your time working on business that isn't going to move the needle and is energy sucking, time wasting and soul destroying. You must have some discernment in where you spend your time.

The easiest way to spot this is to ask yourself, "Does my calendar reflect my priorities?" Your frequency is what you frequently see. Therefore, if your calendar isn't full of big rocks, needle moving activities and what you actually care about, then you're not going to make fast progress. Stop treading water and make the calendar reflect the person you want to become.

Put your non-negotiables in there first, then add the must-do activities to grow your business and then add in the admin. This might be different for every business; networking could be a core component of how you'll grow your business and expand personally, but it must feature on your weekly calendar for it to really be a priority.

The next thing is that you must always have a few game changers that you are working on. You need to be working on one radical big rock, game-changing client at all times. It gives you purpose. There's a magnetic energy and a higher vibration to that kind of business, so push yourself to be a visionary, to think much bigger than you currently are, and seek out the best-case possible scenario. When figuring out what to work on, who to target, always ask yourself this question: if this works, how big could it be? Get a gamechanger in the mix, focus on it and go after it with swagger, knowing that this client, strategy or partnership is so outrageously big that it could change the game forever.

This leads me to the next chapter and an idea that, if put into practice, will magnify your business and your life experience more than anything else.

Remember that is what life is, a collection of experiences, and we want to be able to look back and say "wow, we really pushed the boat out". I can tell you are someone who is going for it, who wants to leave a legacy, to make a difference and go further than anyone in their family has gone before. I'm proud of you. Now let's get to work and do some things your grandchildren's children are going to be talking about!

CHAPTER 1: REDUCE THE FRICTION

TODAY'S DOMINO CHALLENGE

Use the magic formula to create your cold email.

- Personalised Email Header – stand out and connect instantly.
- Explain what it is about – "It would be great to catch up regarding..."
- Hook – "We are helping (clients like you) do X and Y (benefits)."
- Ask for the meeting – "Would you be free (here) or (here)." For example, "This Friday, or some time next week?"

Check out the free 15 email templates at **www.thefirstdominobook.com**. Download them and make them yours.

In your next five meetings, I want you to remain unattached to the outcome, act how the future version of you would act if you'd already landed the biggest client in your sector. Visualise yourself busy, effective, and productive. Cultivate that inner knowing. This vision needs to be second nature to you in your mind. When you're in the meeting you're not coming from a place of hoping, wanting or wishing, it's reality. It's already done. When you are truly busy, you don't chase – you attract by being the person that's on a mission and going places. Have you noticed that when business is rolling in and you don't have so much time, you value it much more, and you show up differently as a result? Develop your self-awareness around how you are showing up in meetings. Keep a log of this and reflect on it: what could you do better?

CHAPTER 2
DO IMPOSSIBLE THINGS

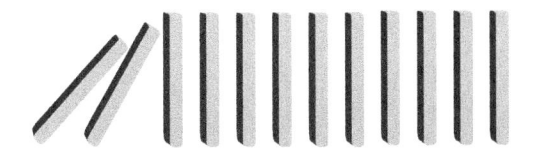

What would be the best outcome that you could imagine? What would that mean for your business, for yourself, for your life?

It's important – no, vital – that you are clear about what the best possible outcomes would be in these domains. Then you can start shooting for them.

Find fifteen minutes today to brainstorm these questions. Really find that clarity.

Now work backwards. Work all the way back to where you are right now. What do you need to do next? Focus only on this step and take inspired action.

For example, as an author it could be a move from selling 50,000 books to 500,000 books a year. A shift like that would bring in more lucrative and adjacent opportunities like: speaking, training, masterminds, collaborations, press, TV, advances for new books, licensing deals, online courses, coaching, corporate affiliations, keynotes, board seats, podcast interviews… the list goes on.

But what's the first step to making this type of exponential increase a reality? It could be something as simple as getting a copy of the book out to every business publication and trade press in the three core markets. It could be getting on to 40 large podcasts and delivering an outstanding interview that left people gobsmacked, having offered jaw dropping and emotionally honest insights that gave value and inspired change. Plant that seed.

Any progress you are looking to achieve starts with one thing: the first domino. Getting coverage in one big magazine, interviewed on a popular podcast, the opportunity to pitch to a business mogul, or an introduction to a key contact – all of them are magnets that pull everything else into your orbit. Securing the opportunity to add value is the win. When you find opportunities to add a lot of value, that's where the magic happens because the outcome compounds.

If we know where we are headed, then all we have to do is keep this burning desire in mind as we take the right steps towards breaking through. The ideas you get when you brainstorm ways to expand your business are the stepping stones to greatness. People get stuck because they want the whole picture right now, but that's not how it works: you have to follow your intuition, have faith in the unknown and do it anyway. The secret is: when you operate from the state of believing it is already done, then you attract. You must embody the spirit of someone who always has more than enough, that way you can be the good you desire rather than just thinking about it. You want to be a cup-overflowing-with-good-things type of person, constantly spotting outcomes that work in your favour.

But what are the right actions, I hear you ask? Keeping with the same example of multiplying our book sales by a magnitude of ten, it could be running Google Search, Amazon and Facebook ads to sell more books, trying to break even and scaling up so that reach is automatically improved. It could be putting out valuable content for 365 days in a row. The actions reveal themselves when you get in this constant state of abundance, and this is your normal default identity.

There are so many ways to take that first inspired step. The first step could be to send a book to *Forbes* in the US, UK and Australia. Or write an email or DM to each podcast manager and share your profile in a unique and differentiated way. Or find an Amazon Ads keywords guru, hire them and test out your theory to climb the rankings.

Whatever it is for you and your business, once you know where you are headed, you have your direction and you act as if it is already done. You ignore your current reality, defying what your senses tell you, and persist anyway, allowing the seeds you plant to have the time they need to germinate. That is how you will make them grow.

You must do it all in a magnetic way, rather than fearing that it won't work. You must take the action, combined with the thought and inner state of it working out, and then go bigger.

Each inspired action leads you to the next, driving you to really push through your limits, aligning your inner beliefs around what's possible and allowing it to be fully realised.

Think about Michael Phelps, the most successful Olympian to have ever walked the earth, with a total of 28 medals to his name. Phelps spoke about what it was like to be in pursuit of his goal, he said, "I went five straight years without missing a single day of workout." He added, "In the world of swimming, when you miss one day, it takes you two days to get it back." Now you may not be going for 28 medals in the Olympics, but what I want you to get is the mindset. He was all in; his thinking didn't let the opinions of others stop him from following what he knew was his path so that he could reach his goal.

For you, focused as you are on landing your first client, you need to let go of the "how" and let the ideas flow, no matter if they seem impossible. Feed those ideas so that they have the potential to generate stunning results. To others, the idea of swimming every day for five years might sound crazy, just like posting content every day for 365 days in a row, recording a podcast, or building a brand. It might be too much for some people. But you are not "some people", you must let go of what's seen as "normal" and do what your heart knows is the thing that's going to carry you forward. Let go of society's perception of the way to do things.

I remember when I first started my podcast. I would get up at any time of the night to record an episode with my guests. It didn't matter if it was 3am in the morning – if that's when they could do the show, I'd be there. The goal was more important than the how.

In playing full out, it allowed me to get bigger and bigger guests on the show. Without the restrictions of a schedule, there were fewer blockages to prevent me from securing high profile guests. I got to practice my interviewing skills and record hit episode after hit episode. The experience enabled me to have transformational conversations, change lives and draw out insights from some legendary authors, speakers, athletes and coaches. It was my personal mastermind group and I loved every second of it.

The only way to move forward is to take inspired action – now. Why does this empower you to open more doors? Easy – the more books you sell, the more people leave reviews, and the more people tell others about your book. You add value by solving problems.

This is the exact same concept for your business. The more people you have recommending your business through word of mouth or by leaving reviews, the more market share you gain.

This is a flywheel that starts you off. However, most founders and salespeople stop because they don't see immediate results, or they pour their energy into the negative thoughts that pop up right before they are about to hit send on the email that could change their lives forever. When you do this, you are literally giving any advantage you created away. It's wasted energy. You are making it harder for yourself. People fear the ideas they have because they might actually work, then they doubt that they are the ones that

CHAPTER 2: DO IMPOSSIBLE THINGS

can pull it off, and this is what stops them from getting the same results as the people that go and take the actions.

With books, they say that the number one title in any category gets the complete lion's share (70%+ of all sales). For example, in the category of negotiation, I am currently at number 10 on Amazon with *The Art of Negotiation*. However, if I can make it to number 1, the payoff is vastly better and there are distinct advantages.

It becomes easier to defend, because the more you sell, the more the algorithm helps to push you higher in the awareness funnel. It works like a flywheel, and when you have momentum, more is more. Just like when you are climbing to the top of a mountain, you have the advantage because you can see further. More opportunities come to you: reporters reach out for quotes in their articles, universities and companies request bulk custom orders, and requests for speaking engagements pick up.

The trick to all of this is that you need to be able to see further before you reach the top, before you have the strategic advantage in order to get there. You need to put the strategy into action before you get all of the pay offs. This works in the same way as investing: to make the most money, you have to pull the trigger before the stock charts really take off. You have to have a vision, and sometimes that vision will seem impossible at first, but you know deep inside something is telling you that you can make it.

"The thing that gives you butterflies, that lights you up. That world you see when you close your eyes. Chase that. With all of your soul, chase that."

– EDDIE PINERO

There is a big reward for getting to number 1 in your field. I want you to be pushing for impossible things so you can attract these outsized returns.

For example, as a salesperson, you are tasked with putting on an event for 50 senior leaders in your space. The purpose is to drive momentum, new leads and awareness. In order to make the event a roaring success, you need valuable content and interesting speakers.

What about inviting the most prominent figure in your industry to come and speak, to give the welcome address or be part of a panel? This would set your event on fire. It would set a new standard for what's possible.

OK, so do you have the person in mind? If so, reach out and plant the seed. It might take 20 emails to get the result, but what if it works? The pay-off is priceless, with intangible value and strategic importance up the wazoo.

Even if you fail, the process builds character and differentiates you and your business from the rest; you are someone that dreams big ambitious dreams and then puts them into action on multiple fronts. It's just how you operate. This is how you set a new standard for your company and yourself. You raise the bar. You go after things others say are impossible.

You miss 100% of the shots you don't take. Do you think I could get James Lawrence (Iron Cowboy, who ran 100 Ironman in 100 days), David Meltzer (*Shark Tank*), Chris Jarvis (*Be The Giraffe*), Annalie Howling *(Unapologetic)* and Eli Harwood (*Attachment Nerd*) on the show if I didn't believe I could *and* then actually send those requests? It starts with one, the first domino, and then you build from there. These guests were not my first domino. They were the eightieth. Where we are going is Ed Mylett, Jesse Itzler and Jon Gordon. Expansion is always the focus. Once you get the first domino, it rolls on from there – but you've got to take the chance and back yourself.

CHAPTER 2: DO IMPOSSIBLE THINGS

These desires for a bigger future you have in your heart, they were given to you for a reason. They are real because they are possible for you. There's a version of you that can go out and make them happen.

One tip I teach my students in negotiation training is to ask for things you don't think you can get. Did you catch that. ASK. FOR. THINGS. YOU. DON'T. THINK. YOU. CAN. GET. It's a skill, and you start practising it today. By making this part of your DNA, to go out and keep pushing the boundaries, you **show yourself** what's possible. You'll see that, once you start asking for things you don't think you can get, you will expand your own understanding of what's possible. When some of these requests are accepted, you'll see that the limitation was only in your mind. It's a strange but exhilarating experience when you first encounter this and see that it's you holding yourself back from your bigger life.

How can you apply this principle to your business today?

- Set a date to run an event, a dinner, a breakfast. I don't care what it is, but invite that figurehead to attend, to be the guest of honour, to do the welcome address.
- Email that radio show host and tell them that you want to come on the show.
- Send in your story to the top 15 magazines or publications in your field, get the editor's name and send it to them. Show them how what you are doing is relevant to a current topic or event.
- Attend networking events 2-3 times a week from now on. Your association will drive unique invites to other events you wouldn't otherwise be invited to attend. Life rewards the risk taker, the person that puts themselves in the path of success.
- Call that client and get an appointment, show value.
- Go to that office building and make the connection.

- Ask for the introduction, referral or contact. Often, all it takes is a name or a small tidbit of information and a whole new line of business opens up right in front of your eyes.
- Make a referral in business that could help someone else, give them your contacts, over-deliver. Put out the energy you want to receive.
- Ask the question you fear asking: how can I get the first domino? What needs to happen for that to be true? Now commit and put into action whatever strategy comes to mind.
- Run the ads, invest in the person, expand to that market, get on a plane and make the time to see the clients that matter.
- You are a mover and shaker; your presence, your belief, and action change what's possible.
- Ask when the contract will be signed. You have value to offer so act accordingly.
- Ask for a fee, put your prices up.
- Ask for coverage, press, connections, references, testimonials, then put them out into the world.
- Ask clients what makes the best service, then iterate and deliver on these aspects.
- Go to the source, not near to the source, go direct to the source. Message every top 50 client target on LinkedIn. Message like a normal person, not an AI scripted chat bot. Be who you are destined to be right now. Don't delay.
- Ask your friends and extended network to like your posts; get over yourself and your fear, and get on with it.
- Your desire to win must be bigger than your fear of losing.
- If you are struggling with cash flow, ask for cuts on your bills, extended payment terms. Get into the habit of finding ways to make what you think is impossible, possible. It's just what you do. Don't think about debt or the situation

CHAPTER 2: DO IMPOSSIBLE THINGS

you are in. Only focus on the feeling of the wish fulfilled. Live in that feeling. Do not put any energy or time into the feeling created by the problem.
- Stop wanting, start doing what others think is impossible. Everything starts to shift around you once you lock in and take inspired action that's aligned with what you would be doing if you already had landed your flagship client.

The cave you fear is the one you need to enter, so live in that cave. Be the light in the darkness. Let your desire to outcompete, outwork and outsmart, burn brightly. That's what keeps you warm at night. That's what gets you out of bed at 3am in the morning to continue working. That's what you need to tap into. You need more exciting things, more asymmetric, unlimited upside opportunities in your life.

When this works, when you pull it off and you land your first client, then EVERYTHING changes. Let the vision and feeling of that happening fuel you. You don't need more sleep, more money, more connections, you need more get up and go and more resourcefulness. Do everything you think is impossible but would be magical if it actually happened.

You should be glad it's hard - that is what keeps everyone else out. Can you see how your thoughts are keeping you stuck? Inertia comes from not trying, not attempting to go bigger because you fear failure, you fear looking silly and being embarrassed. Yet success comes from the exact opposite approach. The win is in that failure, because it's another step towards success and then, once you do win, everything changes.

Dig into that bucket of ideas and keep executing. Write down all the ideas you have for expansion and get them in motion. You aren't doing enough from a place of faith, of feeling that the goal is already achieved. Trust me. This is where everyone falls down. They blame their circumstances, yet that circumstance is happening because they have stayed still and are now trapped in fear, not knowing which way to go or what to do next.

Founders and salespeople who aren't making things happen have allowed their old program to dictate what they can do. In this case, it's quite clear what's going on; it's our mental programming that's keeping us stuck. Simply put, our awareness of what's possible is restricted by our past experiences.

- Old excuses
- Old fears
- Old insecurities

It's all playing out and keeping you operating within the tight boundaries, always limited by your past success.

The breakthrough occurs when we take action *before* we are ready. I know it sounds backwards, but actually it's forwards.

That's the leap. That's what inspires change. New behaviours equal new results. Inspired action is driven by the goal already achieved. You must come from the place of behaving as if you've already secured that dream client. This is a place of conviction. A place of knowing. A place of calm, not fear, dread and worry.

Imagine if you already had your first flagship client. Really get into the spirit of it.

Feel the confidence you'd have knowing you already had the cash flow, credibility and revenue attributed to your pipeline secured under your name. The big breakthrough has already happened; this feeling, these emotions and that rock solid confidence, is where you need to take inspired action from. These ideas you get need to be pushed forwards and acted upon.

Confidence comes from taking the action before we are ready. Breaking out of the old, restricted pattern.

"Do the thing and the thing will give you power."

– RALPH WALDO EMERSON

This is how you generate business expansion and growth.

It's because *you* are expanding and growing.

Doing new things that your old self previously wouldn't have allowed yourself to do causes your old programming to die and new pathways to become stronger. Your mental programming shifts.

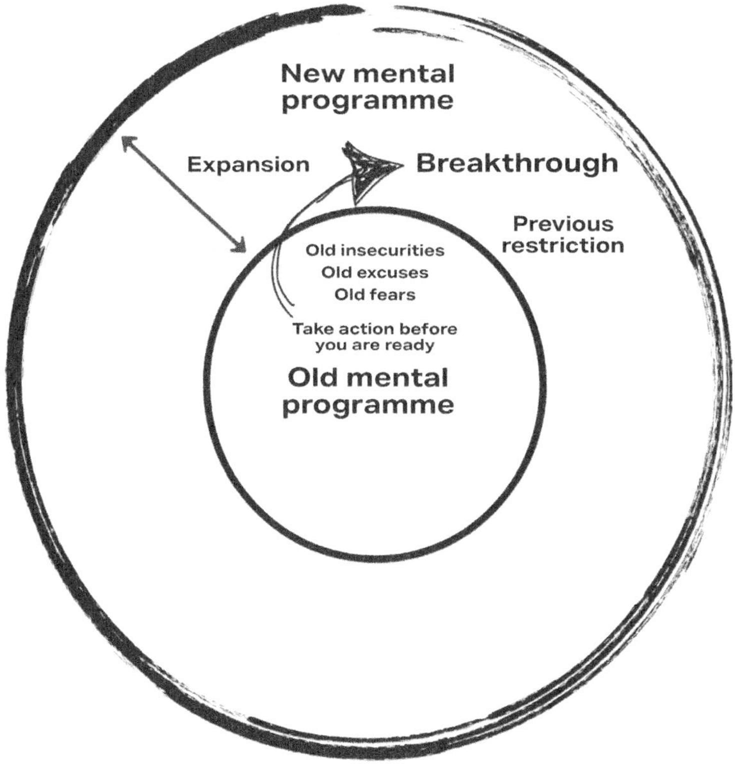
New mental programme
Expansion
Breakthrough
Previous restriction
Old insecurities
Old excuses
Old fears
Take action before you are ready
Old mental programme

It's all possible. Once you figure out the next step towards achieving that first domino, it all happens pretty fast: the script is flipped and then the things you want end up being attracted to you. Don't be surprised that, when you do the things that scare you, everything else you wanted comes quickly as well.

One powerful tactic that most founders and sales managers find impossible is consistency, but you've got to learn to love it. This is how you set a new standard for yourself and for your business.

Why does this matter and what do I mean by consistency? It matters because it's the thing that will separate you in every arena. Be willing to do the thing without any sign of external reward for long enough to get the breakthrough.

This can be sending out those tailored prospecting emails, going to the networking events and the conferences, DM'ing on LinkedIn and creating and posting valuable content across your platforms. This is you in action mode, locked in and executing your non-negotiables. Don't look at the outside results, instead have faith. Most people self-sabotage and lose momentum because they aren't able to be consistent, to follow up on every lead, to make the most of the opportunities that are in front of them. This is what you have to do and keep doing for long enough to see the win; set your intention and don't stop!

Talking about winning, most people (family and friends) won't believe in your business until you win, so stop looking for that validation. Win first and then inspire. Your journey will be testament enough.

This is important, because when it comes to doing things that other people say are impossible, you need to stop living on autopilot and become intentional with your time instead. This comes from your calendar: use it to create conscious awareness of where you are going. Everything should go into your calendar; this will help you stay on track and live each day with intention. It will allow you to slow down time and make sure that you live a life that's fully alive, with every moment feeling powerful and driven by a real sense of direction.

In addition to that, you should block out time for prospecting, for posting and for reaching out for referrals, coffees and meetings. It doesn't have to take long, just 30 minutes, but it needs to happen every day, consistently. You can also block time to read 10 pages of a book that will help your customers. Make yourself invaluable; you have to become better. That's a person that cannot be stopped.

Block out time to review your target client list, to see where you can get an introduction. Don't try to take shortcuts here by outsourcing this part to a firm so they can get you a lead. You have to do it yourself. That's the situation you are in: I want you to win, and I want you to become an opportunity-creating master, knowing that you have everything you need right here. You have more possibilities at your fingertips than you are giving yourself credit for.

Plan in time for adventures, trips and exploration. If you have a partner, plan in time for you to go on date night and for monthly meetings. This can sound weird at first, but as a business owner or sales professional, you've got big dreams to achieve, and you are making them happen. Therefore, why wouldn't you have a monthly meeting to plan out your vision together and your three-month goals. Everything that's important to you goes into your calendar. I go for daily walks with my wife, and this is where we do our daily vision planning for the next three months. It keeps us aligned and also gives us time to catch up on the micro whilst moving in lock step towards the macro. Try it – it works! Manifesting as a team is much more rewarding.

People will try to tell you that it's impossible or that you are too regimented, but it is the exact opposite: because you have it in your calendar, it's a priority and it gets done. This will mean that you are more liberated, have more direction and are living "on purpose".

THE FIRST DOMINO

TODAY'S DOMINO CHALLENGE

OK, take a breath, there are three parts to this challenge and I need you to do all of them in the spirit of abundance and like someone who's just sold their company for fifty million dollars.

Part 1:

Hi Laura,

Hope you are well. Happy Friday!

I will be in Barcelona (insert place) next week and wondered if you had time for a coffee or a catch up?

We're working with BMW (insert client) at the global level to help them with (insert how you help them) as well as improve (insert what you improve).

It would be great to connect to chat more about this and discuss your priorities, if you have availability.

If you happen to have some time on Tuesday, Wednesday or Thursday, it would be great to connect.

Best,

Michael

Send this out to 50 different stakeholders at clients you would like to meet. Only send this to big dogs. I don't want to see you shirking back. Send it to the Head of, the VP of, the CEO of. There is no shortcut. Do this now. You will get a response. You might not get the meeting with everyone next week, but you will start the conversation. You will put yourself on their radar.

CHAPTER 2: DO IMPOSSIBLE THINGS

Part 2:

Next, look at their LinkedIn page and Google them. Where are they speaking? What events are they attending? What industry bodies are they involved with and supporting? Be there. Book it now. Attend the workshop, join the trade association, get into these circles, send them your deck, your company blurb, get on their agenda. Create the magic. Make the connection. You are one connection away from changing your life.

You literally cannot fail to win if you follow this strategy like a dog with a bone. The problem is that most are like a fish out of water with this: they can't endure in this environment; they get thrown about by the tide and the changing demands of each day, and as a result they don't create the momentum needed. They prefer the safety and comfort; they play it smaller than I am suggesting. It's a one, two strategy. You are playing to win. You are here to make a big change.

Part 3:

Check in via WhatsApp, DM or text with three people you haven't spoken to in a while in your industry but would be valuable to have a coffee with. This can be connections that aren't your direct customer but are also selling to the same crowd. Coffee catch ups like this are vital to give you a pulse on what they are finding that is working. They can lead you directly to referral city, where the dollars are flowing day and night and the party doesn't stop. Be a giver in these coffees, see how you can help them. Don't be a leach, be a provider, a valuable asset, someone that's advantageous to know. Over deliver, do what you say you will and move on to the next. Plant good seeds everywhere you go.

CHAPTER 3
TRUST YOUR INTUITION

THIS is probably one of the most important lessons you'll ever learn. However, it's not something where you can say that, once you have learnt it, you've cracked it. It's a skill you need to keep developing throughout your life. As new situations, challenges and opportunities present themselves, you'll have to make choices, sometimes by leaping into the unknown, but there's always this one thing you can rely on.

I'm not sure if you believe in God or a higher power, but it's my belief that learning to trust your intuition is what gets you closer to God. There's a oneness to it. There'll be times that you just have to trust and let the Universal Intelligence divinely guide your path. Napoleon Hill called this Infinite Intelligence.

If you get the sense that you need to be somewhere, do something, or have a flash of inspiration, an inner knowing, then lean into it. Go for it. This is your intuition telling you something. Don't worry so much about the how, just take action; follow the spark of an idea, the passion, the energy, or the champions who support your mission.

Thomas Edison was asked what he would be doing if he hadn't discovered the incandescent light bulb and he replied, "I'd be back in my workshop instead of talking nonsense with you." I'm paraphrasing here, but you get the idea. When you become all consumed with an idea, it leads you forward; having an obsession means you are on the verge of a breakthrough.

The secret to the light bulb was getting the filament to stay alight but not burn completely through. This was done by creating a vacuum within the bulb.

If there's one thing you need to get your business off the ground, it's champions. They are first movers, people willing to stick their neck out and take a risk because they believe in the bigger mission. It can also make them look good within their organisation and for their own personal brand. Find these advocates, because they are your lifeblood, and reward them with your time.

Critically, these champions have power and influence within their companies, and they actively go out of their way to sell on your behalf. Sometimes, depending on the nature of your business, champions will be early adopters who love what you are trying to do. They are your community, and you need to feed that community, stimulate its growth.

How do we find our first champions and advocates? You've got to cross the void and follow your intuition.

My advice is: go direct to the source.

In the early 00's Jack Ma and his team of salespeople at Alibaba went out to visit factories one by one. Back then, these factories in China weren't familiar with working with customers online, let alone ecommerce. Some didn't even have internet access! But this move of going direct to the source was critical and helped them gain an advantage over eBay. They built their business brick by brick, one champion and one factory at a time.

Dropbox found its champions through word of mouth. They focused heavily on launching a huge referral campaign to drive up subscriptions and get customers to fall in love with their product. In April 2010, customers sent 2.8 million direct referral invites! Talk about creating a machine that sucks everything into its orbit. It was one specific thing they did that made all the difference: they created "sharing folders" so when a user wanted to share access, they could also invite others through the referral link. It spread like wildfire. By linking it to something both parties wanted, access to the shared folder, they grew organically with an army of advocates touting for new customers on their behalf. The referral strategy was the key to their rapid growth.

Taking the initiative to build out early communities of first movers that you nurture and invest in to get things moving is paramount.

In the early days of Reddit and Quora, they had a different kind of challenge: how do you start the market for an online forum?

You've built the platform but it's empty, so how do you get people to start to use it and generate the content when you have no people and no content? The answer is: you solve the equation yourself by posting your own questions to create the forum – even if you are the CEO! By posting the questions themselves, and getting staff to answer them, they built up the entire ecosystem until there was enough organic activity generated that they could pull back. Sometimes you've got to be your own champion!

Foursquare grew average check-ins 100k by playing a game at SXSW back in 2010. Not having the marketing budget to drop on a booth, they did what any genius start-up would do and created a guerrilla marketing initiative. The team set up an actual game of Foursquare in the foyer of the conference hall with just chalk and two rubber balls. This created intrigue among thousands of people. They played all day long. When someone didn't know what Foursquare was, they'd have them pull out their phone and show them how to use it. They captured hearts and minds, gave out T-shirts, stickers, and generated a buzz. Genius.

Champions are everywhere. Just today, I saw the President of Stanley respond to a woman whose car had been decimated by a fire. The woman posted a video where she explained that, whilst her car had been destroyed in the fire, out of everything, her Stanley cup was still fully intact. This is where the company president did something smart. He instinctively recognised an opportunity and immediately responded back to the video post with his own message: *"We're going to send you some Stanleys, but there's one more thing. We've never done this before, and we'll probably never do it again, but we'd like to replace your vehicle."*

Now, not everyone's able to donate a car, but if you think creatively, that might be the best $50k you will ever spend.

When my man Jesse Itzler was building his first company he made a calculated bet, a $320k bet to be precise. He only had about $40k in the company bank account, but he knew the payoff could be massive. He got offered four extra special Yankees seats right next to Adidas and the Mayor of New York. Jesse knew this was it, a once in a lifetime golden opportunity. He felt it in his bones and, even though they didn't have the money, they had to bite the bullet and take the risk.

Then they lit up New York; they sent everyone there, and I mean everyone! Their prospects, their clients, their manufacturers, everyone. They all got to go to the hottest event in town because of an entrepreneur with fire in his belly and the desire to make it happen. They had the best seats to the biggest game to give to anyone they wanted to do business with.

On the topic he said,

> "Eminem said it best: 'you only get one shot. Do not miss your chance to blow... the opportunity comes once in a lifetime'.
>
> "I was 25-ish. I knew these tickets would NEVER be available again. Plus, I didn't look at them as just tickets... these seats were some of the best 'real estate' in NY. So... I said, 'WE'LL TAKE THEM'.
>
> "My partner and I borrowed money from a friend to get

the tickets. I don't suggest people go into debt like this, but at this stage in my journey, it was a very calculated bet. And the way we structured the loan we couldn't lose… if we didn't pay back the money to my friend (who was a HUGE Yankee fan), he would get the tickets transferred into his name for life. It was no lose for everyone.

"It was a great deal, a big bet… and boy did those tickets pay off!!!"

When Brain Chesky and the other Airbnb co-founders wanted to acquire their first users, they doubled down on New York. As soon as it took off, they flew there every weekend. In the mix. They would go door to door, taking photos of apartments, staying in homes and putting them online, physically doing the work to grow these communities. This hands-on growth strategy allowed them to rapidly take new ground; when people used Airbnb in New York and loved it, they would take the concept with them back to wherever they came from and spread the idea of Airbnb to that area.

New York was planting seeds for them in other states and, because they carefully and intentionally looked after these communities and nurtured early adopters, they got insights that meant they could iterate and build momentum quickly. The closer they got to their early adopters, the deeper the understanding they got on what new product features were valuable and how they could improve their service. In meeting these needs they were able to create a massive buzz around Airbnb.

Chesky said, "We tried to build loyalty, knowing that if we did that, they would tell their friends. We'd host parties, meet-ups and all sorts of things."

This process created excitement, and what does the press love? Excitement. The more folks that were talking about Airbnb the more they told their friends and the more the press wanted to cover the story. The press was a needle-mover for Airbnb. It brought in more users to the fold, who then told more people via word of mouth, generating more buzz in a new place and bringing in more press.

Back to another Jessie story for a moment. When he started a timeshare private jet company called Marquis Jet, he needed a way to generate leads. Afterall, he needed access to wealthy people, ideally tech entrepreneurs – people that could spend $250k on a 10-hour flight time pass without blinking an eye. He saw that a conference called TED was taking place in Monterey, California and so he decided to go along. He flew in, got to the event, and realised he was going to need a pass to attend. There was no way he was getting past security without one. What did he do? Give up? Turn tail and go home? No, he innovated.

He saw where everyone was headed during the break: the coffee shop across the road. Every hour and a half a wave of people from the TED conference would come over to buy lattes and muffins. The next morning, he woke up at 5am and went to the coffee shop and cleaned them out of muffins. He bought all the muffins. Now he controlled all the muffin inventory.

When a TED attendee would come across from the conference for a coffee and a muffin, the staff would say, "I'm sorry, sir, I can give you a latte but we are all out of muffins." Jesse would swoop in like a magician and reveal that he happened to have an "extra" muffin if they wanted it. Quite ingenious, if you ask me. He saw where his target market was going, saw what they were after, then cut the supply off so that he could gift them to his target customers, which opened up the opportunity for a chat.

"So, what do you do?"

"Well, I run a private jet company."

"You're kidding; I happen to be in the market for a private jet!"

You can see how it works, right? That was how he got his first

CHAPTER 3: TRUST YOUR INTUITION

sale! It came from buying all the muffins at the coffee shop across the road from the TED conference.

The message here is don't wait for opportunity to happen, create it.

As Paul Graham said in his July 2013 essay, do things that don't scale.

> "One of the most common types of advice we give at Y Combinator is to do things that don't scale. A lot of would-be founders believe that startups either take off or don't. You build something, make it available, and if you've made a better mousetrap, people beat a path to your door as promised. Or they don't, in which case the market must not exist.
>
> "Actually startups take off because the founders make them take off. There may be a handful that just grew by themselves, but usually it takes some sort of push to get them going. A good metaphor would be the cranks that car engines had before they got electric starters. Once the engine was going, it would keep going, but there was a separate and laborious process to get it going."[*]

If you've ever read the book *The Greatest Salesman in the World* (by Og Mandino), a chap named W. Clement Stone pledged to buy 10,000 copies to give to his staff when the book first came out. It's bold actions like these that give rise to monumental outcomes, changing the course of history forever. This gave the book a much-needed boost and Og Mandino confidence in his book promotion journey. Millions of copies later, countless lives and fortunes improved, it all started with one champion supporting from the sidelines.

---

[*] paulgraham.com/ds.html

Nurture your champions

Now you have a big group of champions, bring them together and evangelise them. This can be in the form of a newsletter series, podcast or just on LinkedIn. Celebrate them because they are your stars, elevate them and help them to shine by giving them a platform to promote the topic or industry your business sits in.

There are outsized returns achieved by having a team of champions. You'll need to cherry-pick your first target clients, but having these champions gives you proof points, content and references in the form of case studies, quotes and public displays that will then enable you to break through.

Your intuition, and following it when it comes calling, is what stands between you and leveraging this to your fullest advantage.

Go to that city, book those flights, create the conversation. This is level one. This needs to become habitual, instinctive, table stakes. Surround yourself with people doing more of this than you. People whose energy matches the possibility they offer, on a higher plane. You'll see these people because they won't be operating from fear, hope, wishes or stress; they'll be calm, in the zone, taking inspired action, moving forward, making progress – they will have momentum.

Level two goes back to the previous topic of doing things others say is impossible. You need to get to the point that you can spot synchronicities and ideas and take action, no matter what the voice in your head says. For example, if I want to get my book reviewed by the *New York Times*, how could I do it?

First, be realistic. If you're an underdog, own it: maybe you don't have an agent, you're not living in New York, and you don't have connections or an 'in' to the organisation. If that is the case, then you are going to need to *create* the way. So, what do you do? You boldly walk up to the reception.

Your first strategy would be to ask them to send the book up to

CHAPTER 3: TRUST YOUR INTUITION

the editorial director; you never know – with the right time, right place, right person, it could work. But let's say you get blocked, what then? What different strategies could you use?

You've got to extract as much information out of this person as you can without them brushing you off. In the course of your probing, "How would I get my book to this person?" They say, "You could mail it in, but it will just sit in the pile with all the others." You realise that would do you no good: you want to stand out, make an entrance, be seen. "You could try the media room around the corner, but you need a pass to get in and I can't just give you that."

Media room, you say? Hmm, interesting. *This* is your sign. Don't pick up on the no pass situation, pick up on the media room: "What happens in there?"

"It's where everything gets dropped off – packages, deliveries, anything going up into the building."

Boom! You are away at the races. You've got to use what's available to you to get to the goal and outcome you want (and need).

You then take action. Rather than walking away defeated, you go check out if you can find this secret room. You circle around the building and see an inconspicuous unmarked door. It's closed and the red light on the lock indicates you need a pass to enter. This could be it. You hang out there for a few minutes. Don't let your head talk you out of greatness. All that stands between you and getting your goal activated is a random small door. Behind that door is a wealth of opportunity.

Next, pull the book out of your bag, address it to the person you intend to send it to, write a message inside too, and then sign it. This book is going up and you're going to make it happen.

Notice as you are reading this story, a book could be anything: designs, artwork, a portfolio, a CV, your business card, a prototype. It can be whatever it is that applies to you; I am just using a book as the example because that is familiar to me.

And just like that, the door opens – someone is coming out! Instinctively, you spring forward; this is your chance. You catch the door before it slams shut. You peer inside and ask, "Is this the media room? Can I send this up to Julie?"

A voice from the very back says, "Why yes, this is the media room, and yes you can. What do you have for her?"

You calmly and confidently pass them the book, filling out the paperwork and saying thank you before you walk away victorious. There's no need to overexplain, just take the opportunity and move forward. Don't dash your chances of success: you are meant to be there; you have value to give.

I want to add that this will require persistence, possibly more than one attempt with multiple stakeholders. You should be prepared to make your way to that same door many times, not giving up, not listening to that voice in your head, and not letting the fear of looking silly take control. You've got to be a way maker. It's got to become part of your identity.

I'll give you another quick example. It was 5.30am on a random Saturday in the autumn. I was in New York, walking out of my hotel on 51st Street to get a coffee from the Starbucks, when I noticed the Hachette Books Group offices right in front of me. I had one copy of *The Momentum Sales Model* left and instantly the idea flashed in my mind that the book needed to go into that building.

I got my coffee, walked back to the hotel and grabbed a copy of the book. Then I looked on LinkedIn, finding someone there that it might be relevant to (executive editorial director so and so), and wrote a message. I added my details and put together a note that said, "Let's create some momentum together."

After trying all the doors, I found one side door that was open and entered the building. The security guard was a pleasant man, which is not always the case (ahem WSJ). He greeted me with a smile but, despite his positive disposition, he told me that he wasn't

CHAPTER 3: TRUST YOUR INTUITION

allowed to take anything behind the desk. I'd have to come back at opening time on Monday. The problem was I wouldn't be there on Monday as I was flying back to Singapore in four hours' time.

What to do? Was it game over? Hell, no! That book was going into that building: it was meant to be there. I went back to the hotel and casually asked the night manager what to do.

He said, "So this book needs to go back to Hachette, but you won't be here to deliver it?" I was showing him the address whilst he said this; I wanted for him to see just how close the building was to the hotel.

I replied, "Yes, it needs to go there. It has to make it."

He thought for a moment and, as if inspired by another force, he said, "It's just around the block. We'll take care of it."

You need to understand that the option you need is right in front of you. Thoughts can be transferred from one person to another. If I had rocked up and said, "Yo, can you take this book down to Hachette offices on Monday for me?" he would have looked at me like I was a crazy person, probably offering some line about not being able to handle other people's property. However, by providing the context of the situation (I am flying out right now, so I won't be around on Monday, and the details of just how close building was), I planted the seed. It allowed him to come on the journey and, most importantly, make the connection between the solution and the idea. Like a light bulb, once that connection is made, you can feel it; a decision is made and boom... we're on and in business together! Suddenly he's going to make sure the book gets there for me.

It's a seed planted and, at 6am on a Saturday in New York City, it is working whilst I'm not even in town! You've got to create what you want to use. To bring temporary champions along on the journey with you, you need to persuade them through your energy to help you out and, in turn, you need to help others in the same way. Life has a funny way of giving you opportunities to do this. When you put good out into the world, you get good back – it's all about energy. Everything is energy.

When I got to the airport two hours later, the check-in staff explained to me that there was a kid with autism that was going to be sitting next to me. The mother really wanted my aisle seat and she was asking whether I would be willing to give it up. The problem was that I would be trading my aisle seat for a middle seat, and on a 19-hour direct flight back to Singapore (which is the longest in the world at the time of writing), it wasn't something they expected that I'd be willing to do.

I immediately understood this woman's situation and knew what the right thing to do was; after all, her situation was much more significant than mine. I'd happily give up my seat to help her to be with her son and calm him on the flight. It was a no brainer. The staff were shocked that I'd do it, but it made complete sense. Simply put, she needed my seat more than I did.

The point is that you shouldn't do people's thinking for them. You aren't them. So, when you are making asks, put it out into the world and see what comes back. The way you do it is everything. If you are giving, the world will give back tenfold. I can guarantee you. Rocking around the world with a pessimistic "woe is me" attitude, a victim mindset, is a sure-fire way to lose. You won't create any magic. All of which brings me to my next chapter: you've got to be a magic maker.

CHAPTER 3: TRUST YOUR INTUITION

> **TODAY'S DOMINO CHALLENGE**
>
> Get into the spirit of your intuition. I want you to go for a walk and start dreaming again: what is your intuition telling you to do next? When we start down a path, the *how* will reveal itself. Get in tune with your intuition. Go someplace that lifts you up, without distraction. Wherever you find peace, throw some tunes on and go for a run; raise up your energy and start throwing some ideas out there. Then note them down. Put each of these ideas on to sticky notes some place where you can see them. Keep up this practice as you go throughout the next 90 days. I want you to get closer to the spirit inside.

CHAPTER 4
BE A MAGIC MAKER

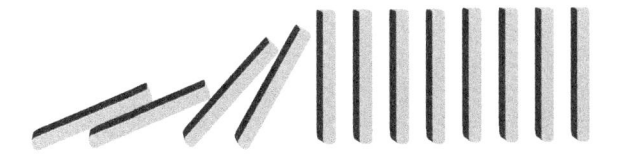

THE way is already written. The outcome is decided. The only thing that matters on this entrepreneurial journey is who you become. You are the key factor. Whether your dream happens or not rests upon your choices. It's down to whether you'll become the right type of person, **the persistent never-taking-no-for-an-answer person.** That is the person that holds a vision with no sign of progress but keeps on giving.

I know I'll become a decamillionaire and more. I know it. It's not a question. I will never give up. I made this commitment after reading *Think and Grow Rich* as a 31-year-old who'd spent time dealing with some things, resolving some past traumas, understanding my self-worth, building my self-belief and ridding myself of what wasn't working. I saw a vision of my future self and I knew it was possible.

You need to decide that it's not a question of if, it's a matter of when. Inevitability is powerful. So, the only thing you need to ask yourself is whether you are committed to doing the work. Are you able to be nimble, flexible, and strong enough to make the sacrifices required? These things might not be what you first imagine.

Naval Ravikant, entrepreneur and angel investor, says there are only four ways to free yourself, the 4 C's of creating leverage. These are: code, content, capital, and collaboration.

Are you able to let go of your creative process and train someone else to do what you do? To relinquish control? Are you comfortable with having a process and training someone else up to do this part of your business, the part that you have always done, the part that would pain you to let go of?

You need to learn how to get money, use money, and manage money. Collaborate. Most people think they can collaborate, but trust me, most people are wrong. When they are challenged, they become defensive, wedded to their ideas and experiences. They struggle to see another person's point of view. They are not flexible or adaptable, and they do not pick up on the skills and genius that resides inside of others. They want to be the star. The problem is that you need people. You need a team to be able to do what you do and, as your business grows, you're going to need to scale the team.

All of these things lead to scaling your business, but you do need them all. You need to be able to see that working harder is not the answer, but working hard and doing the right things is. It's who you become that gets you further. If you are just grinding away, "hustling", then you'll reach a point where you aren't able to drive any more revenue. There just isn't enough time. You're going to need to automate through code, create content to help others, use money to solve pain points and collaborate with many different folks. Are you this person? Could you be?

There's a magic maker in you. I am now going to help you unleash it. The more you give to others and come from a perspective of servant leadership, the more you're going to rise up. The more you put others first, enabling them to grow, and the more you pour into them, the more you will flourish. Once you can come from a place of service, for your team and for your clients, it changes everything. It no longer becomes about your goals, your financial reward, your kudos, your status, your burn rate, your priorities, it becomes about them. This is where it needs to stay.

Nervousness is because you are too focused on you. It's not about you and it never was. If you are nervous about giving a

CHAPTER 4: BE A MAGIC MAKER

sales presentation or a talk or a particular conversation, then you are too focused on you, what's in it for you, how you are coming across, what others will think. This is coming from within and it's holding you back. It limits your capacity. So how do we get more capacity? We flip the script again.

There's going to be a lot of script flipping in this book because it's all about service, so you need to focus on everyone else. The value you give and the person you become is the one who can give to all. Everywhere you go, light up the room, light up their hearts, inspire their story, find the magic in them and pull it out of them.

Those clients you are looking to win, they have magic in them. Find a way to give so they can tap into that magic. The way to do this is by becoming a magic maker. Wherever you go, your intention should be to leave people better off than you found them. You don't engage in gossip, you don't belittle others, you don't categorise others, you see people as they are: human souls, all with their own ideas, dreams and values.

How you operate is of such importance to this whole thing; you must hold yourself to a higher standard. Not one based on what's around you but one that sees the magic in others.

When you are a magic maker, you have the ability to look into the future and pull it towards you, making it possible. Believing it is possible is a cornerstone of this ability. It's part of the formula for success. You are a visionary. This is the muscle you must train. To be able to create magic, you take an idea and go to work. Like an inventor, your belief carries you through the moments of fatigue, frustration and dead ends. You are only one connection, one conversation, or one move away from your bigger future. Once you have your purpose nailed, you can move with swagger, creating magic along the way.

"Are you being you? Are you being true?"

– ANONYMOUS

As the entrepreneur or salesperson in your business, you are the engine, you're the motivation, the difference maker. Your job is to connect the dots, bringing the pieces together in a way that opens doors, inspires action and pushes the boundaries of what is possible.

Think about it: what seems impossible to you, could be another person's regular day. The guy that raises $25m with a quick email and a short pitch deck doesn't bat an eyelid at landing a flagship client, because they expect it to happen. There's an inevitability to it, an expectation and a "yeah, of course we did". To you, you're obsessed with getting just that one client because you think it will then open up the road to a whole plethora of success. In a way, you think your whole company rests on this one defining moment.

The formula to magic is knowing that linear progression - rules, barriers, blockers, the ceiling of what is - can be broken through at any time of the day. When you are around people breaking bigger boundaries as a normal part of the journey, it expands you. Robo taxis, drone deliveries, Autonomous agents, cryptography, it all exists already. We just needed to innovate enough to put the pieces together in a way that made sense to produce those incredible outcomes.

That is to say, I understand where you are at, my friend. You want to believe what I am saying; you want to chill out from your need to close that client because it means everything to you. But I need you to trust me, to trust that your ego is running the show, and we need to dial that down for a bit. I get that your desire to

CHAPTER 4: BE A MAGIC MAKER

have reached that goal already is insatiable, mainly because of the outward success it would project and the subtle *fuck you* it would deliver to every hater and person that doubted you. However, none of that is needed right now. I need you to come from a place of light energy, a place of creation and inward success. A place of knowing. Dark energy is a great motivator, but light energy will get you to your destination faster and in one piece, with an abundance of opportunity around you.

In order to innovate, I need you running on clean energy, in flow with your creative juices, pushing yourself to expand the edges of what you perceive to be impossible and going after it. Think about the four-minute mile. Space exploration. Mars. In a few years, the first manned mission to Mars will happen. It will be a breakthrough. Diseases that affect millions will be eradicated with the use of AI to figure things out in orders of magnitude greater than humanly possible, trend spotting, categorising and crunching billions of data points. Surgeries once impossible will become routine with AI-guided machines. Barriers are being broken all the time through innovation and the pursuit of *more*.

I need you to suspend your disbelief. Let go of your need for it to happen, so that it can happen. I need you to get around bigger ideas and bigger people. Stop making this about you and how this client will prove that you are right. I get all that, but this energy is not helping you land that whale.

What you need is to be cool. You need to be like John Travolta in *Grease*, Iceman in *Top Gun* and Samuel L Jackson in *Pulp Fiction*. Sean Connery as James Bond. Ryan Gosling in any movie. Or for the ladies, Penelope Cruz, Salma Hayek, Kim Kardashian, Zendaya, Gemma Chan, Ashley Park and Ali Wong.

Unflappable. Perfectly them. Sure of all outcomes. A motherfucking, cool-ass founder who's going places, not for the accolades and dirty martinis on the beach, but for the purpose, the mission and what it will mean to solve this problem. The greater good.

The journey. The adventure. The willingness to push past the doubt, putting the dollop of anxiety to the side and saying, "I am all in. I have value to offer here. I am going to go after it as my most authentic version of myself, speaking my truth, getting around high-energy, high-calibre people."

You need to know and expect that boundaries get broken the more attempts we make. If boundary breaking was a daily expectation, it would be natural for us to attempt to break them. We wouldn't wait for the perfect conditions because they'd already be here. I am alive – that's all that's needed to make an attempt.

If trying to do the impossible and make it possible was the baseline, then we'd just do that and not think so much about it or ourselves. As a result, we would experience more flow, more joy, whilst potentially having some worse falls along the way. But you know what we would do at a higher frequency? Make magic and break boundaries.

You need to normalise this approach. Expect to win. Leverage your curiosity, get out and talk to people, have conversations with your customers: would this feature work for you? Would something like this help? Refine, iterate, try again, go out into the field, speak to people, put it out, ask for feedback, move forward. Do all of that rather than just sitting behind your desk hoping that contact miraculously finds its way to you. It's all good to hypothesise, to make the perfect plan, but until you have conversations, collaborate and ask at scale, then you're not going to get as far.

What conditions do you need to make this happen?

To be alive – that's it. You alive? Good. Now go create. We must reduce the gap between idea and execution, between thought and feedback, between slow and on fire.

CHAPTER 4: BE A MAGIC MAKER

Codie Sanchez talks about a lesson she learned from her mentor, Bill Perkins. She asked him why he was so successful. Do you know what he told her?

"The only reason that I'm successful is I'm faster than everybody else."

The lesson is to do it now. Bill says, "By the time they have thought of an idea, taken it to a meeting and started to move, I have already made three mistakes and found a faster way."

Speed matters. Your commitment towards a bias for action – not getting caught up in what might happen, tabling it with others, not waiting until you think you are ready – is paramount to your success and directly linked to the first domino. This is how you collapse timeframes, increase momentum, and dominate a market. I guarantee your leads will go through the roof!

By adopting a bias towards action, you discover mistakes and dead ends faster, you find the way forward by iterating and then ultimately you win. Because you get into action mode quicker and stay locked on finding a way forward, you make the necessary iterations and improvements through learning and conversations.

If you can do what it takes your competitors a week to do in a day, then you can outcompete them. Reduce the time between idea and execution. Instead of waiting for a meeting, call that person right now. Put that idea in motion, do the thing. Find out if it's possible, uncover, create, make mistakes and make the way. The speed you create magic at is magic in and of itself. You now operate on a different timeline to everyone else; you do things in the now. Build that plane on the way down baby!

THE FIRST DOMINO

> "Change is hard at first, messy in the middle and gorgeous at the end."
>
> **– ROBIN SHARMA**

Your first domino is waiting, it is already there. It just needs you to get out there and knock it over. Once you do, three more will come around the corner in quick succession. Normalise knocking over dominoes. Normalise putting things out before you are ready, normalise sending rough sketches, unfinished products and work. Then you can get the feedback, go again and improve, unattached from the need to be perfect, to have it figured out, to have that client. If you already had the client and the confidence, you'd be doing this already. The secret is to do it before this is a reality and then pull that reality into form, much like a magician. Except, all you did was think and behave in a certain way and it produced an outcome. That outcome can be repeated, scaled, anticipated.

Prepare the way for the success you envision. Create the opportunity in the CRM system, then get ready because that client is coming. Prepare as if it is going to happen – because it is.

If you knew you were going on holiday, if you'd booked a flight, then you would pack up your stuff and get ready before the flight took off, because you knew it was going to happen in the future. It's the same here: prepare for your target client to arrive because you know it is on the way. Book the celebratory restaurant, create their account in your system, get that contract prepared, have a meeting about how to provide the most excellent customer service and onboarding for them. Prepare the way because it is happening.

CHAPTER 4: BE A MAGIC MAKER

Have you ever been so absorbed in what you are doing that time flies, your sense of self disappears, and you are just in a state of oneness? Have you ever had that? Maybe it's when you are coding, designing, or writing. This is where we need to get to when we are building the sales engine of our business: self disappears and the optimal conditions are created because you are feeling good, everything you touch is turning to gold and you're being brought to life. You are vibrating highly, and you can feel it: the words are flowing, the points are being hit, you are landing with your clients and you're feeling awesome. This state of flow is the unlock. This is where you capture the client's heart and mind. You are in a state of high performance, your energy is abundant, and it feels like you could keep going forever. You get more done in 30 minutes than you have on some days. It's a magic state and it is the key.

Flow is like turbo charging your brain. Like nitrous oxide in your system, it gives you superpowers. Your memory, productivity, collaboration, intuition, and creativity go sky high.

Can you see how the art of the possible is maximised? You are on fire and you feel it. You aren't focused on yourself, instead you disappear and you focus on the task at hand. You are in the zone, operating at much higher levels of thinking.

Then you must infuse this state of flow with your creativity, using your ability to harness that purpose and direct it at will. You've got to get your Jerry Maguire on, when he's fighting to keep his last client, Rod Tidwell, and everything under the sun is going wrong, what makes the difference? What changes his stars?

It's not the desperate asks, the pleas for a favour. No, it's a rhythm, a truth, a connection, a love of the game, a desire to solve his client's problems. He is fully connected to his why. The first domino is an adventure. There are going to be twists and turns, but remember that you are a lighthouse, leading the way for others to come. Most of all, you inspire people through your actions, your ability to see them, to be naked. (I'll explain that last part in a minute, but you do need to really see people!)

Your clients need to feel that you are there for them. You can be passionate about what you do, letting it guide you, and even fall in love with the process, while solving the client's problems.

Go deep. Have unwavering faith. It needs to be done in your mind, so spend time in that vision of what it's like when you have a full book of business. Picture that time when you are turning away clients because you are too busy, that time when you're expanding on all fronts. Spend time in this place in your mind, where you can live your dream realised. This place exists, this desire was given to you for a reason, because it is possible for you to realise it in the real world.

The only thing you have to remember is that you must get out of your own way, get nakedly honest about your limitations and then go to work on growing in the right areas. Move the needle. If there's something that scares you, but you have a hunch that it will move the needle, you have to be prepared to get naked, to get honest and to go do it anyway. This is the muscle that needs to be developed. This is where you can take the blinders off, and your biggest ambitions can become a reality because you transform into the type of person you need to be to do it.

For all you parents out there, you'll know what I mean when I say that everything changes when you have your first child: it's like you've been looking at the world one way, then you suddenly realise that there's this whole other version of the world. It's 360 degrees, a whole new perspective and a whole new level. You need to level up, and you do this by failing and learning, failing and learning. Over time, you get better, you find your groove, you become a parent pro, you become a master, but it doesn't start that way.

I think being a dad is the coolest thing. It's awesome because you start it at an age when you've got most other things figured out

CHAPTER 4: BE A MAGIC MAKER

and then you have this child that you need to understand how to operate. This image of yourself that has to change and adapt, you have to step into it. It's the same with sales and closing that first client: you have to step into it. You have to get out of bed ready to rock like the badass you are. You have to take that bottled-up magic and let it out. You have it within you. It's in your attitude when clients reject you, when you compose those prospecting emails, when you need to get your message out to the world and you're fearful of what 'the world' thinks.

The power of letting go is exemplified by an exercise in Navy Seals Training. It's called Drown Proofing. In this crazy challenge, instructors tie your hands and feet and throw you into a three-metre pool.

Yes, these are the world's elite forces, but can you imagine what that's like? You're sinking to the bottom of the pool and the objective is to survive for more than five minutes with both your hands and feet bound.

The panic is too real for some and they have to be rescued. Sadly, others have died. The paradox is that the more you struggle and fear the outcome, the more oxygen you burn. You don't succeed by treading water like you might think. The way to overcome the challenge is to fully relax, drop to the bottom of the pool and use the floor to push up towards the surface again. Once at the top, you take a gasp of fresh air and float to the bottom again, before repeating this motion for five whole minutes.

How interesting is it that the reality of this exercise is the more you try to stay alive, the more likely you are to die.

Knowing that people have died before doing it also heightens the need for mind control. The idea that you have to completely let go and let yourself sink to the bottom in order to get back to the top and get your reward (air) is nuts.

It's the law of nature in reverse. The concept suggests that the more effort you put in, the less reward you get. It can be like this in sales, especially when hunting for the first domino. You think that because you go all out, and struggle and fight, that it's got to happen. However, in reality you are not taking advantage of the situation and you'd be better off worrying less.

When you are too concerned about the possibility of failure, you restrict the options available to you. Your mind closes the door to strategies that will actually keep you alive. This is all about playing freely, reaching your full potential and taking risks. Dropping to the bottom of the pool to push off again back to the top feels like a risk in the moment. Relaxing seems like a risk. Not caring about the outcome seems like a risk. However, when we stop caring about failing, it opens us up to success.

The way to move through this, to get better at this, is called exposure therapy. You need to put yourself in situations where you can fail and practise relaxing, being OK with the outcome and enjoying the process. When you train your mind to be calm even when the situation is dire, you execute regardless. You do your thing and that's where you win.

When you are afraid to do something, lean in and get after it. Navy Seals, the elite performers, go through this level of training to help them in the world's toughest situations. Imagine what you could be like if you took a bit from their world and applied it to yours.

On the topic of letting go, during the writing of this book, I came across a post by Musa Tariq, current Chief Marketing Officer at GoFundMe. I'm paraphrasing here, but it told the story of his first job growing up in London. His mother owned a flower shop and his job was simple: every day he was to water the plants and make sure they thrived.

One day, there was a delivery of six Birds of Paradise (these look like a big orange bird with a spiked comb on its head, for the

CHAPTER 4: BE A MAGIC MAKER

non-horticulturist among us), none of which bloomed. Every day Musa went into the store and made sure they had the essentials: sunlight, water and food. After three weeks, five of the flowers had bloomed, releasing forth a beautiful display. However, the sixth flower struggled and, as a result, did not sell.

One day, he had had enough and decided to throw it away. As he was doing so, his mother came out and delivered a knockout lesson that we can apply to sales. "What are you doing?" his mother exclaimed.

"I'm throwing it away because I think this one is broken."

After examining the flower carefully, his mother went back in the shop and came out with some scissors. She began cutting away some of the green leaves. Musa was confused. They were healthy leaves – wasn't she going to kill it?

His mother carried on and said, "In order for us to grow, in order for plants to bloom, sometimes they need space. They need light."

The point here is that sometimes we need to let go of the things that are holding back the light in order for us to bloom. We need to create that extra space.

What leaves do you need to shed so that you may flourish? It could be people, thought patterns, jobs, limiting beliefs, too many commitments, or trying to be all things to all people.

It's funny because, looking at the flower and the green leaves wrapped tightly, you'd assume it was doing well, but in fact, it was bound up and needed to be freed in order to fully stretch its wings. What is life telling you that you need less of? It could be saying yes to everything, gossip, mindless scrolling on Instagram, social media comparison, fear of failure, playing small, being controlled by what people will think.

Don't kid yourself: this is all playing out in your business. All your hang ups and your ability to thrive depends on your willingness to get vulnerable for a second and decide what to cut away.

83

Once freed, you can go more directly to the source. I am going to share with you one needle-moving activity that you can make your mission whilst you are trying to topple your first domino. That first domino falls because you are considered an expert in your field. This client is willing to overlook the fact that you are a relatively new business, that you don't have all the case studies and logos under the sun. They look past all of that because you can bring something that others can't. You offer flexibility, innovation and the ability to hear their problems so you can customise the solution.

In you they see fresh air and a chance to make a real difference. To them, you are a ray of light. The more you can step into this and become that ray of light for them, the more you can own your space and become a leader in it.

What you think is your biggest disadvantage (not having any big clients yet) is actually one of your biggest advantages. You get to service the hell out of the first client you land. This whale of a client isn't going to know what hit them; you're going to overdeliver and keep on overdelivering until the cows come home.

So, how can you maximise your chances of success? First, you must know what you stand for. This is so you can find and select clients that align with your values, business goals and ability to deliver in droves. There's no point making this more painful. This is you evaluating them too. Remember, as a small team or company, you can be nimble but you can't be everywhere; resources are your bottleneck so you want to make real sure you are hopping into bed with the right client that will make this a mutually beneficial relationship and propel your business into the stratosphere.

Next, learn how to use humour as a lubricator. Most don't because they are too focused on business and, as a result, this serious one-track mind blocks opportunities for real connection.

CHAPTER 4: BE A MAGIC MAKER

They are missing a trick. When you can relax enough to enjoy the process and bring your true self to the party, then you can actually start to build a better relationship with your clients and cover more ground. When you stay surface level, keeping it all about business, it creates a barrier that is felt, even if it's not openly spoken about. It keeps the relationship transactional, one dimensional and basic. Humour can lighten the mood; it can inject some fun into the proceedings and give you an edge when it comes to standing out and being someone that they would like to work with.

Where you are really heading with all of this, as well as building a trusted relationship, is to get to the point where you can influence the decision criteria of the client. When they go about making the checklist of all the things they need to consider when selecting a partner in your space, you have to ensure that their checklist is robust.

You want to ensure that your differentiators, the thing you do better than anyone else, are included as a check box on the list of required capabilities. This puts you miles ahead because, when the RFP or RFI comes in, you've got a strong case that is also already bought into by the client. The client understands why your points of differentiation are valid, valued and a must have.

When you reach this level of influence with the client you have transformed from an ordinary vendor to a trusted advisor. You must always keep the best interests of your client at the forefront of your mind. It is demonstrated best in the scenario where you are able to say, based on what you've told me and the outcomes you are looking to achieve, we don't have what you need, but I know a company that does. This is the ultimate form of trust: when you are doing right by your client, not taking every piece of business and trying to shoehorn your product into a space it is not meant to fit in.

The mistake that begets most average salespeople is that under pressure they tend to chase after every piece of business. This message of becoming a trusted advisor goes out of the window. It's quite disturbing what the need for internal validation and a revenue target will do to some. Be mindful as you drive momentum, selling to more clients, that you aren't slipping in the area of your integrity. Not everyone is a fit, and that's OK; not all customers will be on the right timeline. Instead of letting your fear and desperation cloud your judgement, step back, take a breath and ask yourself: am I doing this because it is right for my client or because I am under scrutiny? Clients can smell fear and desperation; the trust is only built when you maintain your steadfast commitment to guiding them in line with the goals of their business.

In contrast to this, when it is the right client and they are ready to play ball, the way you win the RFI is to go to the source and influence the decision criteria before the RFI is even sent out. How do you do this? You are the expert. You give value to your client by openly sharing questions that they should be asking potential vendors in your industry. These questions naturally line up with your strengths and defensible differentiators whilst highlighting areas of capability that you competitors don't have but your client now understands they need.

In sales methodologies like Command of Message and MEDDIC, these are called trap setting questions. I recommend you listen to the episode I recorded with John McMahon (the godfather of MEDDIC) and five-time CRO as it will provide the context and go into detail on more of this (the link is at the back of the book).

This is an extremely powerful way to build the narrative with your champion. This is where you build your champion: you arm them with information that not only makes them look like a professional (i.e. they are doing their due diligence) but also

CHAPTER 4: BE A MAGIC MAKER

shows that they are committed to finding the best solution for their organisation. Once this new criteria makes its way to the Economic Buyer (the person who has the ultimate decision-making power over the deal) and your champion can articulate the benefits, then you will be in a much stronger position.

Never assume you aren't competing with another party. The deal is not yours until that paperwork is signed and, even then, you shouldn't take your foot off the gas.

Ask your champion straight out, are there other companies and solutions also in consideration? What are we competing on? Is it price? ROI? Resources? Is there any internal competition from departments offering similar solutions? You need to know what you are up against as early as possible.

A solid tip to take action on right now is to create your trap-setting questions sheet that track back to your defensible differentiators.

Traps questions sound complicated, but they aren't, so there's no need to let them overwhelm you. All they do is identify your competition's weakness and point back to your unique differentiators and areas of value that the client may not have considered. These questions are not to trap the client, instead they trap the competition by highlighting and getting buy-in around your differentiators (DD).

These questions lead the customer towards understanding how your DD helps them to get an increase in revenue, save costs or decrease risk. The components of a well-designed trap question come from outstanding discovery. You don't tell the client about all the things that will happen if they don't have your differentiator. You get them to tell you about what happened previously. In a Force Management podcast on this topic, John Kaplan said, "Think about what questions you would ask the client to get them to contemplate your differentiators."

This is where the magic shift occurs. For example, if you work for a data company with a lot of granularity, freshness and scale of first party data signals, you know all the issues and difficulties that clients face when they don't have rich first-party attributes. Many of your competitors claim to have accuracy and scale but you know it's hot air. Therefore, you want to get this point across and have your client recognise the importance and premium nature of what you have to offer. To do this, don't tell them about all the bad things that can happen if they don't have your data set, instead have them tell you about all the challenges they experienced instead.

By having the client articulate what happened the last time they worked on a project that required your differentiator, they sell themselves. Get them talking about the pain, say something along these lines, "Tell me about a time that you were trying to enrich your first party data set. What challenges did you have with third party data sets? What impact did this have on the business?" Then ask, "What are you doing to ensure that you are working with partners whose data set is scalable and has the granularity required to increase the match rate?"

Keep it light, this is nothing more than normal discovery question mode. You're drawing out insights for them to recognise the impact of not having proper criteria around the differentiator which you have, on various outcomes and departments in the business.

CHAPTER 4: BE A MAGIC MAKER

DD	Trap questions	Trap the competition
Often centred around something that builds trust: propriety, technology, code, IP, it is a distinct advantage that prevents or protects.	Often focus on accuracy, methodology, adoption, frameworks, granularity, speed, network effects, exclusive partnerships, acquisitions (e.g. what impact did not keeping accurate data have on your ability to generate useful insights?).	By focusing on the challenges of not having the differentiator you have (e.g. a strong methodology), it highlights their weak methodology that allows them to take shortcuts. It is not rigorous, or up to standard. Now the client recognises how detrimental this is to their business.

Remember, "people rarely argue with their own conclusions", that's why, if we can get the client to a place where they understand just how valuable your differentiators are (and that they are required), it moves the entire conversation towards your business.

To emphasise this, you should put your beliefs out there by making them open source; it should be on your website, and easy to find. Put your trap questions out there, post about it (e.g. five questions you should ask your supplier). Publish case studies that highlight your exact differentiators, (e.g. generating 656% ROI). Why X is a critical factor for any CMO.

Add value by helping clients stay ahead and be better informed.

It has a ripple effect. You are leading the industry, you are the expert, and the expert showcases how it's done in all forms. You are a source of knowledge: clients look to you for understanding, to further their own discovery. Therefore, you must be willing to put it out there, document your journey as it evolves, set the standard. That's how you become a leader in the industry.

You set the standard and, as a result, you get to advise the client on how they might want to think about your solution. This way, when the RFI comes in, you wrote part of it and can provide solid answers and rationale as to why it matters. This is where you start to influence the decision criteria, ahead of time, planting seeds in the minds of your potential clients about things they might want to be thinking about, or criteria to include. Once it is identified as required, and the conclusion has been made in the mind of the client, you are well on your way. The ability to have access to influence this part of the sales process only occurs because you are a person of value, integrity, and good character.

Why do winners always win?

I absolutely love this topic. Why do winners always win? It's because winning is a habit for them. They have mentally programmed themselves into winning; even when they lose, they don't dwell on it for long. They learn from it, maybe make a few tweaks to their presentation, delivery or story, in the process of continual improvement, but that's it. To winners, losses are not permanent, they are not defined by them, they don't let the loss take them over mentally. Instead, they see winning and losing as the same thing; they are aggressively neutral towards how they treat winning and losing. Their temperance is the same: if they win, they are neutral; if they lose, they are neutral. When they experience a loss, they operate with the attitude that this happened *for* me, not *to* me. This is an incredibly powerful tool

CHAPTER 4: BE A MAGIC MAKER

to program yourself to make winning a habit. This is how magic makers operate, and it has to do with their thinking.

The winner's mentality

Inner state of knowing, positive expectation and possibility

Success

I'm feeling neutral, everything is working in my favour and supports my growth

Neutral, unattached to outcome

Failure

I'm feeling neutral, everything is working in my favour and supports my growth

Losers, on the other hand, can be spotted a mile off; when they win they let their emotions get too high, and when they lose, similarly they let their emotions get too low. They are all over the place, rocked by the external event, trapped by ego and identity based on the outcome.

As a result, they are constantly thrown about by life's sea of changing situations. In contrast, winners have the same temperance regardless of what is happening on the outside. They develop their inner potential and release it; they are constant winners because it is a habit.

The loser's mentality

Emotions follow
external outcomes

Success

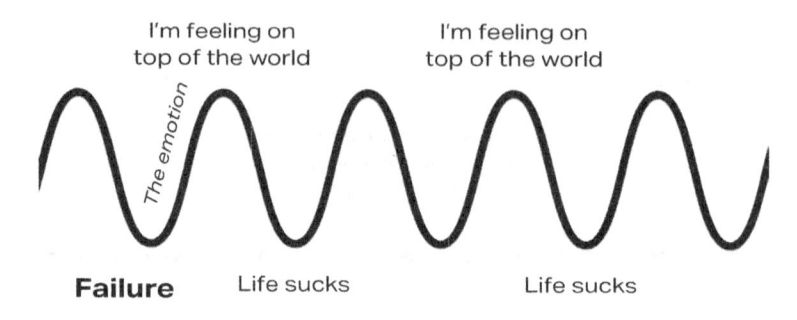

I'm feeling on top of the world

I'm feeling on top of the world

The emotion

Failure   Life sucks   Life sucks

Develop the habit of winning today by controlling how you think about the circumstances that come your way.

A client is not responding: "It's happening for me, not to me." A client doesn't understand your proposition: "It's happening for me, not to me." A client reschedules last minute: "It's happening for me, not to me." Can you see how, each time, this is an opportunity to engage with abundance and take advantage of the opportunity that has been created? When a client blows you off, use the extra time to send out some more prospecting emails and make some calls you wouldn't otherwise have made. When they don't understand your pitch, ask questions to find the exact area that is making it difficult to understand and then refine your presentation to match.

Everything is an opportunity to win, except when losers focus their attention on the unreal. They make up a story about what's

CHAPTER 4: BE A MAGIC MAKER

not working for them, or why it's bad, and as a result, they accept the idea that this is somehow a bad outcome. They make the unreal real through their thinking. When we detach from our need to control the outcome, we instead create space for the good in our lives to flourish. The vacuum is filled with abundance, with new ideas, connections, and possibilities.

How do you attract your ideal clients to your business?

In the same vein, you've got to study your top clients. If you don't have any clients, look at someone else's best clients in your company or industry. Look at your competitors' best clients: what characteristics do they have? What do they have in common? What are the trends? What is this type of ideal client all about?

When you know this, and you can clearly articulate who it is you want to work with - your ideal client - this is where you must focus your marketing activity. You need to communicate and market to them in a way that resonates with this exact person. This way you'll attract more of the same. Birds of a feather flock together and all. It's true, where are these ideal customers hanging out? What are they doing day to day? The likelihood is that there's a high chance more of your ideal clients are in the exact same places, attending the exact same events, on the same bandwidth and frequency.

Put yourself in the heart of the action. Go to lunch at that restaurant every day for a month. Study their LinkedIn pages from a year ago, what events were they at? What societies and clubs are they a part of? Clients are creatures of habit - show up, be there, start to be a familiar face - familiarity, even from afar, brings down the walls of resistance, and the spark of an idea can be produced.

"Hey, maybe we should grab a coffee."

"Let me introduce you to so and so."

It can come from anywhere; the point is that you are purposefully putting yourself in proximity to the environment where your ideal customer lives.

TEST NEW STRATEGIES TO GET ENGAGEMENT

THE CRO of a company you'd like to work with releases a book, so buy it, read it, promote it and tag them. Create the conversation by supporting what they do. A potential client has a side hustle they started, they launched a beauty product, so buy it, share it, support it. Show up. You act differently to 99% of the masses by just supporting and advocating.

Try hitting up anyone that has spoken at the conferences in your industry. These folks are likely more inclined to enjoy the spotlight and therefore have an increased likelihood of engaging with you. They may not be the right contact, but that doesn't matter, because they can introduce you to someone who is. They too want what can make them look good, so help them shine.

They enjoy their status - it strokes their ego a little bit that you would reach out to them - and then they can help you by introducing you to someone in their organisation (as long as what you have is valuable; this must be the case). It must be of value to the person they are introducing you to for them to look good, or else you are just wasting time and they won't respond, which means that what you say when you reach out is of vital importance - you must hit a home run, they must get what the value is that you offer and make the connection (even if it is subconsciously) to them making an introduction and them looking good. Stroke this ego a little bit, using this psychological tactic to open more doors, making others look great. You increase your influence and become a valuable person to know. This goes back to the chapter on getting an epic life; you want to be an interesting person, involved in valuable projects, and someone these contacts want to stay close with, to follow along.

You've got all of this inside of you. Now it is time to bring it out. Keep the winning habit, attracting your ideal customers and experiencing the flow, and your ability to break through and penetrate organisations from multiple different angles with ease.

> **TODAY'S DOMINO CHALLENGE**
>
> What can you action today that you are putting off or allowing to take a week? Do it now.
>
> What do you need to pull the trigger and move forward with, even though you don't feel fully ready? Could it be a project, proposal, meeting, or a conversation. Do it now.
>
> What old patterns, behaviours, stories, processes, habits and limiting beliefs do you need to let go of in order to take yourself and your business to the next level? Do it now.
>
> Get out there and create more magic in a day than you have in the last month! I'm telling you it's possible. I want you to prove it to yourself and radically change the speed at which you take inspired action on things.

CHAPTER 5
GET AN EPIC LIFE

PEOPLE, clients, anyone with a heartbeat, they all want to be with people that are doing things. You've got to have a thing. I don't mind if it's running marathons, climbing mountains, skydiving or knitting, but you need to have a thing. You are more than one dimensional. You can't be all work. You need to have something you are passionate about that makes you you. It's a differentiator. You're unique, special, interesting, mysterious, a baller.

This is important for a number of reasons. It gives you stories and it gives you depth, which makes you memorable. As author Bob Burg pointed out in *The Go Giver*, "People want to do business with people they know, like and trust." Be kind, have integrity, be different. That's what I am teaching you. Go to that kickboxing class, do that week cycling through Thailand, play the game from your heart. Because that's what matters.

Jerry Maguire started winning, and started inspiring people again, when he took action from his heart. Yes, he made moves from his heart. The whole of life is energy. When you do things that bring you energy, you'll get an abundance, with energy 1+1 is not 2, it's 4. The way to win in business is to love the process of creation in what you do, and to tap into areas of life that you love. That means you will draw energy from the weekend you spent climbing a mountain in Bali, or writing that book, or recording that podcast, and you will put it into your client relationships. You speak from the heart. You want them to win, for them. You have value to offer, but you are there to connect the dots, to help them by creating the most value for them that you can, in whatever way that is.

The perfect storm comes because you show yourself to the world, you win hearts and minds and inspire the right action when you authentically let people in. Naturally, you understand the client's world, and their pain, and they feel heard. This is because your core intention is to listen to understand, not just to respond. This absolute focus on understanding makes it easier to pick up details others miss. Are they feeling fearful? Do they get that you'll be there for the long term and that your solution is the right one? How are they making decisions? What's riding on this for your client? What happens if this doesn't go well for them? When you share who you are, you become a real person, your humanness opens up the dialogue and transforms the conversation.

Getting an epic life helps you *need* the sale less and gives you more angles to connect with people on. This energy is attractive. A person on a mission in business and life is an exciting person to be around. This is where the buds of a real business relationship are formed. You can't fake it.

When you aren't afraid to lose the sale or make mistakes, you're free, and in that freedom comes the creativity to get to the heart of the matter. You can boldly explore and collaborate with a client because they can tell you have their best interests at heart.

Due to this, you ask questions that other sellers wouldn't. You poke holes in your own shortcomings and offer up areas of improvement. You are real with them about the potential risks or downsides of working together, and this honesty brings them closer. Your differentiated way of handling the sales process sets you apart from the rest of the hungry wolves all spouting the same jargon, making the same claims ("we're the best in the industry!") and boring clients to death.

If you're a startup, especially if you are a startup, there are

CHAPTER 5: GET AN EPIC LIFE

going to be roadblocks and bottlenecks that you didn't anticipate, but you win based on your ability to convince the client that, when they occur, you'll be able to navigate them together rather than running for the hills. You win because, rather than pretending they're not going to happen, you address them head on and proactively provide a plan of action to mitigate the risk. This is a demonstration of your character, values and heart. It shows you aren't just here for the pay cheque but to create something better, to move the entire industry forward, to disrupt and create real customer value. It backs up your company story, your mission and purpose, and gives credibility to the fact that you are committed.

The risk with a client coming on board with a startup is that they'll have doubts and start asking themselves some questions. Are you going to be here next year? Do you have what it takes? The worry is that, if I fight for you internally and get this approved, and then you disappear when the going gets tough, it's my neck on the line. But it helps if you can point to other examples of how you show up when the going gets tough:

- You run marathons.
- You complete triathlons.
- You compete in Ironman races.
- You strength train five times a week.
- You set yourself mini challenges.
- You travel to diverse places.
- You experience a rich life.

These are all signals to the client that you are here to stay. That you have sticking power, resilience and grit, and you have your client's back.

How you live your life is a signal to the world. If you are a hot mess - not loving your life, angry and hostile, seeing the negative, complaining about the traffic, or the weather, seething about inflation, or your investors, gossiping about your friends, lamenting about your family etc – this is a signal to your clients. It's not just what you do in business that counts, it's who you are throughout your life that matters. How you do anything is how you do everything. If you drive like a greedy maniac cutting people off and jumping red lights, what's to say you won't take the money you are given and invest it recklessly or with too much risk.

Remember, they are the ones taking the leap here. You need to *be the standard*; your daily life needs to reflect the best version of you. Therefore, you are living a rich life jam-packed with fulfilling experiences and beautiful memories; a big life, *is* the key to the vitality, vigour and stamina that confirms and commends your character in business.

There's no playing it small. It all matters. How you do anything is how you do everything. As coach, Ben Newman says, "My definition of winning is YOUR ability to look at yourself in the mirror at the end of every single day and know that YOU gave it your very best."

Ben's philosophy is that you win by attacking your standard. If you keep raising the bar, then the results take care of themselves.

Think about it: if you want to be a high performer in business, then you must be intentional about your life and the standards you have. It's about going the distance, creating advantages for yourself and, whilst this also applies to business, it's underpinned by how you operate your daily systems.

When you have a strong personal standard across your mindset, fitness, wellbeing, nutrition, sleep, relationships, spiritual connection, reading and gratitude towards the things you currently have, it gives you the confidence and the permission to go to places with your clients that others are afraid to tread.

For example, when you pose a question that your client really should be asking but isn't, and you put it out there because it's the right question to ask, then it shows integrity. A choice made without the sole intention of pointing them towards your products or features. Most people ask questions that lead the client to their solution so they can yabber on about how fantastic it is, but they fail to go below the surface, to tap into the psychology of their client and uncover what's really holding them back.

It's so easy to talk about your solutions, your world, but what about them? What's in the back of their mind? What do they need to overcome? Where are they wanting to go? What fear do they have that's not enabling them to fully commit? The answer, and the key to convincing them, lies within them.

It is when you do the right thing, rather than taking the shortcut. It is when you own where your business is at and you share *that* journey authentically. You don't influence through force, trickery or hiding the truth. You attract because of who you are, and how you help the client to work through their shit. You create a safe space for your client to be honest about how they are feeling, what happens if they mess up and this deal isn't run properly or they haven't done their research well and they get grilled on the specifics of why they chose to go with your company. You have to be the guy or girl that is there for them in that moment, to reassure them that they are making a great decision and give them the confidence to feel sure that the plan is water-tight, that you will be there for them.

This brings me back to the purpose of this chapter on creating an epic life. There's a perfect flow where you achieve success the right way, and it comes from loving what you do and loving your life. You've got to have a rocking lifestyle. It's important. Lifestyle is the goal. It's the ultimate achievement. That's what this is all for. So why not start living your ultimate lifestyle now? Otherwise, you are sending a double binding message, when you imagine living an awesome life in the future you subconsciously signal that it will always be in the future. "I'll do this one day. I'll be this person one day."

Fuck that. Today is that day, you rockstar in the making, so get out and play big, live the life you want right now and attract everything you ever desired because you are making decisions and thinking from that place on that level. When you act as the person you want to become, and you think on the same frequency and make the same decisions as that person, you allow that life to unfold for you.

That's who clients want to do business with, someone who is emitting high energy at all times. So let's stop waiting and get an epic life.

In chapter two, where we looked at doing things that other people think are impossible, we discussed how the barriers we face are in our minds. It's our perception and interpretation of life that controls how we experience it. Remember this: someone out there is living the life you want, achieving the things you want, and not letting the labels and society's rules define them. They are doing it right now. They have the autonomy, the travel, the wife or the husband, the self-belief, the rituals, the self-care, the worthiness, the healed inner child, the friendships, the experiences. That's not to say they don't have to work on these things, but they have chosen to start living as that person today, meeting that standard.

In the movie *Point Break* (2015), Luke Bracey plays the character Johnny Utah, an extreme sports pro turned FBI agent sent out to catch the bad guys. As it turns out, they are being paid by some rich dude to achieve the impossible. They take on daring stunts such as skydiving into an underground cave in Mexico, completing the world's first air to earth transition. They also base jump from the top of Mount Everest and are towed onto 100ft waves by jet skis right after the swell from a huge storm in Biarritz, France.

CHAPTER 5: GET AN EPIC LIFE

The point is that what was previously conceived and understood to be impossible is being challenged on a daily basis and, in some realms, this is the accepted norm. For example, in the arena of science, there is an expectation that we will find a cure, new ways of revolutionising treatments and maintain a commitment to the constant pursuit of breakthroughs. Whereas, in normal everyday life, at the societal level, it's less so; breakthroughs are deemed rare and impossibility is lorded as fact.

However, when you flip the script and infuse this idea into your life - that breakthroughs are possible, that going after what you want is normal - and start living as you wish today, you bring the aura of innovation, creativity and spirit of belief into your life.

To achieve this, you want to be around this high frequency energy, allowing yourself to feel alive in your soul. To chase big goals and live at the edges of your capacity.

Ed Mylett regularly references the phrase *"extremity expands capacity"*, which means the more you push it, the better you get at finding ways through, over and around problems. This, however, means finding ways to get into the flow state. It's here that you can accelerate your trajectory. For example, as a writer, I am often woken at 12-3am with ideas. If I wake up and start writing, these ideas take me into a state of flow, and I may write for one or two hours non-stop in a place of creativity, purpose and aliveness. This energy may then go on to feed me with positivity, abundance and possibility for the whole day to come. Therefore, harness these moments of flow - don't ignore them. If you wake in the middle of the night with a light bulb moment, write the idea down, send that email, reach out to that person, do it in the now and make it habitual. Get in touch with what brings you to life and do more of it. This is how you infuse the spirit of possibility and wonder into your life. It's how you live your truth and not the truth of others. Breakthroughs come because of who you are, and it's then driven on by your ability to weave it all together in your own special and unique way, forging a lifestyle that pushes you to achieve more, to live out your full potential and to capitalise on this essence of life.

Sometimes we need to break out of the mould to reset it. That's why you must be purposeful with your time and actively plan in new adventures. If you don't plan it in, it doesn't happen. I find seeking out new places for four-day trips (Thursday – Sunday) so rewarding, or even just walking in new areas. Embracing new things is inspiring because it releases you from the old pattern and allows you to set a new, more expanded one. Everything that exists between your ears is telling you something, whether it is possible or not possible, whether it can be done or, even unconsciously, you don't believe it can be done. Therefore, we must get on the right side of this and control and curate our thoughts to align with the outcomes we want to see in our lives.

I've included a chapter on "getting an epic life" because this is what gives you life. Without being clear on the lifestyle you want to live and starting to live it now, it will always be "someday". Chasing someday is no way to live. Starting today, you must live as the person you *want* to become, to take actions as *that* person and get out and move through the world as that person.

This is not to say that it won't require hard work, or that all you need to do is to get into a good vibration and everything will work out. Far from it. This is to prime you at the core identity level so that the way you operate daily is in harmony with who you aspire to be. Living with this energy will help you to boost yourself up the mountain of success.

Think of it like a computer game; life is a computer game and the more you can surround yourself with possibility thinkers, people doing more than you in the places you want to go, the more you will absorb and think like them. Then, by knowing thyself and putting time in your diary to do the things that give you energy, you have a constant recharge going on. Think of it like you are playing Sonic: when your energy is depleted and you need a boost to go faster, you pick up the rings and they propel you forward. At that point, you are off to the races.

Being in the energy of passion, creation and flow in any domain will give you more energy to apply to your business and the sales you want to achieve. Instead of working yourself to the bone and using up all your energy, grinding harder, you've got to take an hour and do something that lights you up. It will be in these moments, when your brain is off topic, that the idea will suddenly pop into your mind like magic.

This is how you set up the game of life so you can win and keep crushing levels. Levelling up is part of it and you will learn a lot about landing your first client from this process. Not to spoil the surprise, but it will be more about letting go and not trying to control the outcome than you think. Instead, it will be about sticking with it and making it work by being resourceful, whilst keeping your mindset in prime condition.

Getting a life also helps you ask questions about other people. You have an interesting life which can then help you to understand others and probe deeper with them. There's a spirit to someone who is defeated and one dimensional and a certain energy to someone who's just loving all aspects of their life. Who would you want to do business with? An energy of momentum makes things happen.

People make the mistake of thinking that if you are all about business then you'll do more business. Whilst there's an element of truth to that, I believe you'll do more business if you are all about *people* instead.

That's why becoming a master networker is a game changer and now networking never has to be awkward because:

THE FIRST DOMINO

▪ You have an exciting life with a range of topics you know a lot about – you are interesting because you are interested in the other person. The most interesting person in the room is the most interested, so let your curiosity flow, get people talking about what they love, and you'll see the stories appear. Which leads me to my next point…

▪ The more you let them open up, the more personal stories they are going to tell. Stories are literal connections. When someone is sharing a story really listen to them, don't let your mind wander. You can't be thinking about the football score, Netflix, or what your mum said to you about picking the kids up next week. Be fully present and engaged, helping them to add colour and bring it to life through the inspired questions you ask. The questions you ask will demonstrate how well you have been listening and whether you have been paying full attention. When you are all there, listening deeply, the other party will notice this and feel differently and more positively towards you; they will feel heard and, in feeling heard, they will share more. This is where you will stand out to them. They will be drawn to you because you gave them your undivided attention and they will like you even more. The truth is that everyone else is just thinking about themselves, how they are coming across, but not you. You are focused on hearing the other person and then adding to the conversation in meaningful ways, peppering it with openness, enthusiasm, high energy and curiosity.

When they ask, "what do you do?" or "what line of work are you in?" the main thing you need to let them know is how you can be of value to them. To do this, simply say I do X and I help people achieve Y.

CHAPTER 5: GET AN EPIC LIFE

Make it fun, exciting, pour your enthusiasm into the delivery. Don't just say I work in IT, or I run a software business. Say, "I help people transform their productivity at work."

"Oh shit! How do you do that? I think I need some of that in my life."

I am hanging on your every word because you aren't regurgitating the same old crap that everyone thinks they need to say. You are not a pre-programmed robot. You are refreshing, energised and alert, ready to engage with about topics that matter to them. The other part of this is people feel more invested in you when they help you, so give them something they can help you with.

Bonus points: if you can link in a couple of lines about your story and demonstrate a deeper more personal side (for example, "I'm an author. I saw people struggling with everyday negotiations, leaving so much value on the table, so I decided to help to change that. I wrote a book on the art of negotiation and how to get what you want every time. Who knew it would become an international best seller?").

This should be smooth, like a knife cutting through butter. You should relish this question, finding joy in it because you are planting a seed in their mind, and you are CONNECTING! Always have physical business cards to hand. Don't fall for the electronic QR code connection: get in their pocket and in their LinkedIn. Think both.

If asked "how was your weekend?", don't be bland, boring, and forgettable. Instead, endeavour to stand out by answering honestly. If you had an awesome time, say something along these lines, "It was outstanding; we went up into the mountains and did a wonderful hike in nature. You know it's times like that when I feel so centred, and the view was just stunning!"

Or if, alternatively, it was a challenging weekend, you can share openly, "It was pretty tough. I met an old friend and they had just lost their father to an aggressive disease. It really puts things into perspective: life truly is a gift and time is short so we better make the most of it." This is you being real, and it invites the other party to reciprocate the openness. It takes the relationship to another level seamlessly.

If you want to become an outrageously successful networker, it is dependent on the quality of your questions. If you ask a poor question, you can expect a poor answer in return. Ask an open-ended question, like, "I'm curious: what got you started in this field?" or "How did you hear about the event?" and you're going to set the conversation off in a whole new way. Remember, if you want to be extraordinary then you are going to have to do things differently. You can't expect to achieve ten times the results by being the same thing in the same way as everyone else. But this is where the magic happens; it's in having the ability and strength to pick a different path, to choose to be different and expand yourself. This is called growth. Fitting in is no longer an option. You are on the path towards becoming extraordinary at networking and making lasting, impactful and meaningful connections with people.

The thing to remember when selling, networking or engaging in any type of interaction where you want to authentically connect is…

IT'S NOT ABOUT YOU!

Telling stories, connecting, listening to understand, making sure the other party feels heard, this is where you leave the masses behind, and they're all skills that you can master.

But what is it about networking that makes you really uncomfortable? We've discussed how to handle the introduction, now we've got that covered, let's talk about setting boundaries and how to exit a conversation with grace and poise.

I GET IT!

People fear networking because they fear they will get "stuck"

CHAPTER 5: GET AN EPIC LIFE

talking to the same person when they really want to work the room and meet a greater variety of people, making a greater variety of valuable connections. Yes, you guessed it, there's also an art to ending a conversation politely. If you ever get stuck in a conversation you don't want to be in, the way out is simple. Just say, "Well, this has been wonderful. I am so glad to have met you. I promised myself I'd meet five different people tonight so I need to go and make good on that promise to myself. Thank you and let's meet again. I'll drop you a note about coffee."

Just handle it with grace, be confident about you and your priorities and set it in motion.

Alternatively, you can frame the next question you ask so that it indicates the end of the conversation is coming, say something along the lines of "before I go grab another drink, can I ask you a final question… (pause for effect and get agreement). Then ask your last question.

This brings the conversation to an end naturally in a way that gracefully demonstrates you are deeply interested in them, whilst also signalling your intention to move on.

Your standard in this area will get you into rooms and conversations that your business doesn't warrant yet. Never be afraid to strike up a conversation. It taps into a skill that salespeople continually underestimate, which is the power of artful communication and connection. This is emotional intelligence in sales on fire! This is where you apply your EQ. Those that master this in an extraordinary way can literally make things happen that others can't. You are one introduction away from changing your entire life. What's stopping you from getting after it? As Sara Blakely, the Founder of Spanx, says: *"Don't be intimidated by what you don't know. This can be your greatest strength and ensures you do things differently from everyone else."*

The tenth chapter of this book goes into the daily operating principles for being a magnet for success; this is about consistency and routine. First, before we dive into that, I need you to do the groundwork. To figure out *how* you want to live, big picture. This is part of getting an epic life: we need to get clarity around where we are headed directionally.

In 1974, Steve Jobs went to India for seven months in search of enlightenment and, after doing a lot of random shit, he came back with a deep understanding of transcendent wisdom or "prajna". This means trusting your gut. Now I'm not suggesting you jet off to Goa for half a year, but I am strongly advocating – no, mandating – that you do something. It could be that thing you've been putting off that you know deep down will lead you closer to living an epic life today...

> "Have the courage to follow your heart and intuition. They somehow know what you truly want to become."
>
> **– STEVE JOBS**

TODAY'S DOMINO CHALLENGE

I want you to plan and book an adventure or an epic challenge. I know it seems crazy; you're out here trying to land your first domino, why would you need to go to Egypt to discover the ancient pyramids? Or go on safari to a remote part of Northern Zambia? Or spend a week at a silent retreat living with Monks? Or host a dinner party? Or get ripped to compete in a Hyrox event? Why, Tim?

CHAPTER 5: GET AN EPIC LIFE

The point is that it makes your life richer. Experiences are what matters; they make you richer at the deepest level. The time will never be right. You need to take the bull by the horns, get out and live and come back and crush it. If you're savvy, you'll be able to combine winning new business with this task.

The idea of how you will be able to do this will pop right into your mind. Plan to run a marathon and invite a prospect to join you, train together and build a relationship. Create a memorable morning for ten of your top potential new accounts by organising an off roading experience on quad bikes and then have a workshop to strategise how you could collaborate. Combine adventure with business. Be different and you can live the life you dream about now.

This is about getting creative. Northern Lights – booked. Iceland Blue Lagoon – I'm there. *Game of Thrones* tour of Croatia – certainly. Trekking through Himalayas – sign me up. MMA membership – yes, please. Ice bath session tomorrow morning – all over it. TedX Talk – applied for. Podcast appearance – locked in. 75 Hard – challenge accepted. Tokyo marathon – ready! Life – I'm yours!

This will help you to let go of your "need" to land your first client, whilst making you more attractive to everyone you come in contact with. People want to be around people who are making it happen, who have something about them. When you love yourself in this way, pushing the boundaries of your comfort zone whilst being grateful for all that you have, you've won at life! It's an attractive energy, if not the most attractive.

CHAPTER 6
QUESTION EVERYTHING

No really, you should question everything. Whilst you are out there planting seeds, there are conversations with current prospects that you should be having but aren't.

This is where your desire to win should get acutely focused. Hone in on this one part. How useful are your meeting notes when you look back at them a few days later? Are you asking the right questions that uncover information that's valuable for your business? Are you moving the conversation into trust-building territory?

Questions are the linking factor; questions link to relationships which link to trust. It sounds simple, but questions help you to uncover, expand and grow your knowledge of how you can serve your key customers. Why then do so few salespeople and founders get this part right? Top performers don't assume or guess, they probe and keep on going, they are skilful in the way they weave in questions that don't always feel like questions yet reveal information that's valuable.

You need to become a question machine. What conversations should you be having and with whom? Likely they are right in front of you, but you've passed up the opportunity because you didn't ask the right questions and now you think it's a dead duck. To be specific, you have prospects in your pipeline that you have disqualified because they said no, or that now wasn't the right time, but if you'd asked different questions, you'd have found out information that would have led to different outcomes. What you say matters. The questions you ask matter.

This is a distinct competitive advantage. If you want to shine within your business or gain an edge, improve your ability to uncover valuable information and build trust with your prospects.

Questions are powerful because they open up the door. These conversations are what ignite beautiful business relationships. This is what leads to you landing your first rockstar client.

By the end of this chapter, you are going to become a super communicator.

Here's a few tips to get you started. They are the fundamentals of becoming an outstanding conversationalist.

When the client tells you something, make sure you repeat it back to them and ask if you got it right. This process helps to create a positive feedback loop. Someone knows that you were listening to them by how you respond, so when you build this action into your process you, in turn, improve the chances of hearing each other and the other person feeling heard.

You can say something like, "What I heard was you're looking for a complete refurb of the downstairs, a remodel of the kitchen and all the windows replaced. Have I got that right?"

This provides the opportunity for clarification, refinement, and alignment. It all leads to filling the bucket of trust.

The problem is, conversations are energy intensive. It's hard to stay focused with all of the sights and sounds, distractions from mobiles in our pocket, and not to mention the chatter in your own mind for your own thoughts (all 60,000 of them per day). It takes real conscious effort not to get off track and into your own mind. Our strong tendency is to be overly focused on what we are going to respond with instead of paying full attention to what is being communicated.

Communication is everything. It's the non-verbal cues, the

body language, the smile, the frown, the fleeting facial movements, the posture, touch, appearance, gestures, tone and eye contact. It's all telling you something, but we miss so much of it because we allow the noise of the world and our minds to take priority.

The compounding factor is that of the 60,000+ thoughts we have during the day, research shows that 75% of these thoughts are negative and 95% of these thoughts are repetitive. Talk about being programmed! So, here's the challenge: even though you understand logically what you are up against, I am going to need you to apply disciplined mental focus to retrain yourself so that you can choose positive thoughts. Being selective about what you allow yourself to give attention to will then allow you to also focus on the non-verbal communication used by both yourself and the client.

To help you do this, here's a formula developed by Albert Mehrabian who was a researcher on body language. I want you to remember the 55/38/7 Formula. Albert found that the components of face-to-face conversation were broken down as follows: 55% non-verbal, 38% vocal, and 7% words only.

The 55/38/7 Formula

Words 7%

Body, facial expression, movements 55%

Voice, modulation, tone 38%

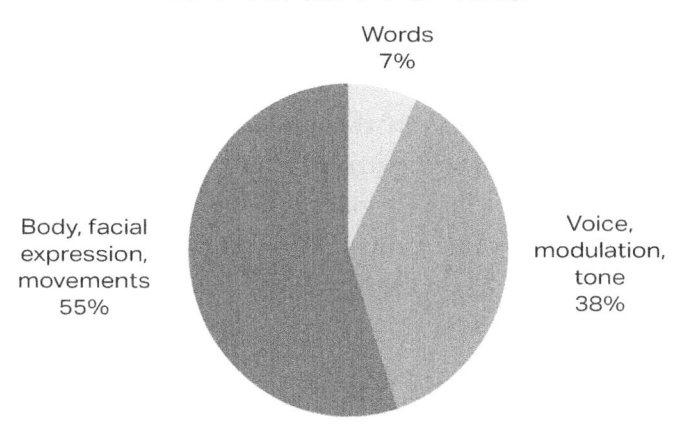

What does this mean? It means that 93% of what you are communicating and what your client is communicating isn't what's said, but *how* it is said: the pitch of your voice, modulation and pauses, your arms, facial expression, body posture, and stance. Combine this with the 45,000 negative thoughts the average person has each day, and you see how emotions, noise and distractions can derail us from connecting and communication can get messy. That is unless we make a commitment to focus on improvement daily.

The next area of improvement is when a client is speaking and sharing key details with us; through the overuse of minimal encouragers we tend to interrupt and break the flow of discovery whilst they are literally unpacking and revealing important details. We think we need to demonstrate that we are listening and encouraging the client to keep sharing but, because we overuse them, they provide more friction for the other person to have to navigate. These are sometimes referred to as minimal encouragers.

You think it shows you are listening when you say "Uh-huh" every ten seconds, but instead it disrupts the train of thought and the authentic expression and depth of discovery. Others include "yes", "OK", "I see", "got ya". Conversation is a process that goes deep if mastered, but so often we barely touch the surface.

The main intention for any client interaction or conversation should be to understand what the other person is telling you. This is the purpose. This is what super communicators keep to the front of their minds. A world class communicator has the discipline to engage in a conversation and make the other person feel so special by how they listen. The questions you ask in response to what the other person has said will demonstrate this and reaffirm your level of attention and focus.

All you are trying to do is to understand how this client that is sat in front of you sees the world. What's their lens on it? How is it from their perspective? But so often we let the opportunity to do this slip through our fingers because we inadvertently take the spotlight and shine it back onto ourselves.

A client might open up and share something vulnerable with you, like I am falling behind on my quota, or I am having a hard time with my manager, or my wife is sick right now and, instead of meeting this vulnerability and showing support, we steal the spotlight. Often, I believe it is in an attempt to show that we understand. However, we do it incorrectly because we fully take the limelight and therefore steal the show. When the client opens up and says, "I am falling behind on my quota", don't say, "Yeah, me too. This market is tough, and they want 45% growth." Instead, say "I understand how that is. Tell me more about what they are expecting." Then the client will open up with new information. At that point, you say, "That must be challenging. Based on what you've told me, here's how I might be able to help." This shows you have reflected on what they have said. This is all empathetic communication. You are holding space for them to share openly.

You've got to know what the client is looking for; this comes down to knowing what type of conversation you are in. Conversations come in three forms. According to Charles Duhigg, author of *Supercommunicators*, there are practical conversations (what's this really about?), emotional conversations (how do we feel?) and social conversations (who are we?) and all three can be happening over the course of one conversation. Charles argues that, "If you don't know what kind of conversation you are having, connection is hard."

The thing to understand is that if the client is in an emotional conversation and you respond with a practical conversation focused on the solution then you'll miss the opportunity to connect, and they won't feel heard. We must match the conversation we are in.

If the client shares "my wife is sick right now and we have a new baby that's two months old", don't say, "I remember when our baby was two months old. It was a nightmare, but we used this incredible pre-school to manage the workload. I can introduce you." You've made their moment of vulnerability about you. Instead of a practical response to an emotional revelation, you need to match it with acknowledging their vulnerability. Say, "That sounds hard. Tell me more. What's going on with your wife?"

This opens them up; it offers an opportunity for them to unload and to share safely. This is what creates trust. You are providing an environment of psychological safety for them to release. It's here that the client reveals who they truly are. These are bonding moments. This goes for any conversation you are having. It doesn't just have to be a client: it could be with a friend, a partner, a family member. It's all playing out, all the time, and a super communicator matches the conversation they are in. Practical conversations are focused on solutions and action, emotional conversations offer a chance to be vulnerable, and social conversations give the opportunity to share our identities.

This is all about hearing each other. If we both match, then we hear each other and the bridge to trust building is established.

The feeling of closeness comes when we go beyond the surface level. This is especially important for anyone in sales. If you are wanting to connect, one strategy is to offer up some information first, reveal who you truly are. When they ask you "how was the weekend?", instead of saying "it was fine, thanks", or some other bland cookie-cutter explanation, you say "you know what? I went on an insane quest to find a rare breed of dog for my children because they fell in love with a puppy that was supposed to be given to us but instead got given to a different family." Then you pull out your phone and show pictures, take them on the journey, let them in, and in return they will do the same. This opens up the conversation instantly and it signals to the other party that anything is OK to be talked about. By you revealing some personal information first, it automatically brings the other person closer. It signals to them that you are allowing them into your world. It allows the conversation to open up quicker and with more vulnerability. The beauty is that by doing this, they will reciprocate and then away you go.

It's there that you get them to open up by asking the right questions, questions that dig into their values, their identity, and their emotions. "Tell me, why did you get started in this business?" or "What was the moment you knew you wanted to do X?" These questions probe the soul, they open up the heart and allow the light in others to break free and to shine out. This is where your magic comes forth; you see others as a gift and you recognise their light. Doing this makes them feel truly special and it will transform the depth and quality of your relationships.

When we ask questions about experiences, memories, and passions, we tap into the root of who someone is at their core. It's this process of going beyond the surface that bonds people and, in doing so, you'll uncover information that most salespeople will never get. The revelation of these insights will change how you do business. You'll get to the heart of why someone thinks the way they do, how they come to the conclusions that they have, and the basis of their opinions.

Questions that tell you more about a person don't always have to be about business. They can come from any angle as long as they allow the person to open up and share.

"What's the biggest risk you've ever taken that paid off?"

"What's the craziest adventure you've had? I bet you've got some stories!"

"When you're not doing elite performance coaching, what do you like to do for fun?"

When you understand the power of asking the right questions, it's a game changer of the biggest proportions. As humans, we like to share on a deeper level and be understood – it just feels good and right. This is the humanness that you need to bring to every conversation. Mediocre salespeople don't know how to do this well and that's why they repeatedly fail to uncover the insights and build the trust required to move at speed.

In sales, you have to remember that most clients have a terrible experience of salespeople. They come to the conversation expecting the worst; they have distrust built into their perception and preconceived ideas of what your intentions are and how this conversation will go. That is, until they meet you. You are going to show them a new way, to open them up and connect through really making them feel heard.

You are going to meet them where they are at, in their world and find out more about who they are at their core, where their belief systems come from, and what experiences have shaped them deeply. Sales is so much deeper than people think, and it's being an expert communicator that makes all the difference – to the strength of your network, the health of your trusted relationships and the bonds you create through how you treat others. Set the world on fire, light it up with your skill in making others feel heard. Recognise the light in them and you'll change the very nature of your results.

As I am sure you get by now, this is an unlock to accelerate. This is where exponential growth comes from; it's the difference between stagnation and expansion, being held back and being blessed. You'll uncover things that others take years to find out – you'll connect the dots and have beautiful friendships form, ones that are lucrative and beneficial, in the harmony of partnership and the spirit of truly knowing someone.

We are humans, so be human. Remember your job is to learn as much as you can about this person, to understand what they are telling you and to meet them where they are at. This means unpacking their fears around what might go wrong as well.

Now, let me share some questions that can help you navigate the sales conversation so that you a) end up with information that is useful, b) go deeper and c) put yourself in a much more advantageous situation to close them if it is right for them.

Buckle up for a masterclass in the right sales questions to ask. Here we go.

Broad open-ended – to uncover

UNCOVER with broad open-ended questions, like "what's going on with you these days?" This gets the conversation started and creates the opportunity for connection and rapport.

Specific – to probe for areas to help

THEN become more specific, with the intention of either revealing pain points or aspirational outcomes.

- What kind of opportunities do you see for improvements in this area? For example, marketing (this can be process, efficiency, results, service, education, profitability, retention, awareness, time management). It gets them to reveal where they need help or what's currently a point of frustration.
- What's held you back from reaching your goals, (whether revenue, targets or KPIs)? This shows you what matters to them and the potential blockers internally and externally.

Questions to uncover motivations, evaluation criteria, and impact

IMPACT-DRIVEN questions like those below are an excellent way to give yourself an edge or move someone closer to committing.

- How do you think the executive team or the board will evaluate the success of this project?
- If you could make this happen, what would it mean for you personally?
- What won't happen if you decide not to move forward with this? This gets them to articulate out loud the risk of not doing anything and creates urgency and rationale around not sticking with the status quo.

Future-oriented questions – to inspire and gather influencing factors for a successful partnership

THIS is one of my favourites, maybe because I am an eternal optimist.

- Imagine it's three years from now and we're celebrating a successful partnership. What would have to happen to make that so?
- What does success look like for you personally? This opens them up to share with you what matters to them. Is it a promotion, more responsibility, or a different motivation they care about deeply? If you get this right, they will share their dreams and aspirations – you'll be surprised what revelations you get.

CHAPTER 6: QUESTION EVERYTHING

Targeted insight questions

IF you want to gain insights, then ask targeted questions that challenge and then probe for justifications to see if there's any errors in their thought processes. Perhaps they have been told incorrect or misleading information by a competitor or have a blind spot that your expertise can help them uncover. This naturally reveals an area for you to help and demonstrate value.

Why is this your strategy? Why do you see that working? Why do you say that? How do you know that? Be careful, though; this inquisitive questioning style must be said with the right tone or you'll likely come across as rude, aggressive, and arrogant.

Practise these first before firing them off. Your tone is vital, it must be curious and soft. Anything else will cause them to close and you'll look like a gigantic pompous ass who thinks they know it all.

Diagnostic questions

WHEN you want to bring it home and get more diagnostic as to the specific pain point or reason, then you can use a closed question.

- Do you think you're doing all you can to... (mitigate, protect yourself from, encourage customers to, reduce, produce, scale up, insert your area of focus)?
- Do you think (X) is a problem for you? (Insert the thing you help them solve.)

Conversation continuation questions

WHERE I see a lot of salespeople get stuck is when there's a natural pause in the conversation; it feels like all the questions have been asked but you know deep down you didn't get any real meat on the bones. You want to keep asking questions but you're not sure which ones. You are all out of options and now you and the client are just staring at each other awkwardly, not sure if the meeting is over but not wanting to be the one to say it.

Where do you go from here?

Well, it's easy.

Simply say "Can you tell me a little more about (insert area you don't feel you uncovered enough detail on)?"

Filler statements

OR, when you get really skilled at this, all you'll need to say in response to their statement is "how so?", or "can you expand on that?", or "go on", or "tell me more", and you can jazz it up by putting a filler statement in front of it to make it even more fluid.

Fillers like, "now you've got me intrigued, tell me more", or "you're kidding, how did that turn out?", or "no way, that is incredible, what was the outcome?", or "that is so interesting, and what would you say is the biggest factor they are struggling with?"

There are so many ways to keep a prospect talking and opening up. Sometimes you just need to keep going because all the good stuff is on the other side of the right question asked at the right time.

I know you got this. You are primed and ready to go out and become a highly skilled question master and conversationalist, making it look effortless and letting it flow with ease. It'll feel completely natural and you'll just have fun. The key is to practice, practice, practice, with everyone: your landlord, your barista, your husband, your hairstylist, the cab driver. Everyone is an opportunity to get better and improve.

CHAPTER 6: QUESTION EVERYTHING

Alignment questions

TO clarify and get alignment, which is important to move things forward, you want to say something along the lines of "before we part ways, can I just check that I have got everything? We covered X, Y, Z and these are the next steps. Did I capture everything or am I missing anything?"

It is important to remember that this is *not* an interrogation. These questions outlined previously are here to guide your conversation as it takes twists and turns. Most salespeople will mess this up. They will think "roger that, Tim" and go out there and hammer their clients with questions. This is **not** what I want you to do. If you've been on the receiving end of one of these salespeople, you'll know what I mean. "Can I take just 30 seconds to tell you what we are all about, blah, blah, blah. Do you find yourself with these issues?" On and on like a non-stop sushi train of verbal diarrhoea that you're being force-fed and you didn't even ask for. It's the worst!

There are two ends of the spectrum when it comes to question asking as a tool: not asking the *right* questions and then slipping into overkill, or spray and pray, firing out more questions than a semi-automatic rifle. It's just as bad, if not worse, than asking the wrong questions, because it shows you only give a shit about yourself. It's selfish to ask too many questions because you need them to tell you what's going on. Leaders do this incorrectly all the time. They know which questions to ask but they do so in a way that sounds more like a demand, and they haven't done anything to prepare the ground for the right conversation to be had.

You must be skilled, knowing when to ask the right question and delivering it with the correct pace, intonation, energy, inflection and genuine curiosity and care so that you can unlock the treasure box. You've got to earn this level of skill; it won't come just because you have the knowledge, but it will come because you got out there and practised every damn day!

When you have insatiable curiosity, you get answers that no one else will discover. If there was a gun pointed at the head of your nearest and dearest, you would find a way to have more conversations, to land your first client, to make it happen. How much more motivated would you be if the stakes were higher than they seem now?

It's easy to think that the more people you touch the better the outcomes will be. Whilst the volume of interactions is important, the key to it is the high-quality pipeline of opportunities that you nurture, and by nurture, I mean have robust in-depth conversations with so that you can build meaningful relationships.

This is a high-leverage skill. It means that you have the ability to open doors and then ask questions that draw out crucial information that you can use to inform your product roadmap, go to market strategy, marketing, sales positioning, ideal customer profile and much more. It is so important. It allows you to adapt your use case, refine your sales pitch, inspire your company's growth trajectory, and fuel the next phase of your innovation.

Often, it's the message that you need to sell. You need to inspire curiosity from your target audience, get them to lean in using the various types of questions mentioned previously. Therefore, you want to be relentless in how you go about putting out your message to the world.

The more conversations you are having, the more lenses you are able to apply to seeing how your product or service can help someone. Why does that matter? It matters because it can help you with how you market your product. You can use this information to showcase and speak to the various use cases that your product has helped solve.

The mistake salespeople and entrepreneurs make is that they

CHAPTER 6: QUESTION EVERYTHING

go all out for the big launch of their company or a new market and then they go back to the day-to-day grind. Instead, you should always be Day 1, always be in launch mode, always be pushing the envelope. This keeps you hungry, it keeps you looking for ways to win the hearts and minds of people you haven't even met yet. These people sit in the realm of customers that find out about you because of word of mouth.

If you want scale, you've got to get beyond just meeting your first customer: it's all about word of mouth. It's the story of your brand and your company, and what you did for the industry. This is the magic; you can keep pushing your message, planting seeds, having conversations, building relationships, going further and, just like an explorer, you will cover new ground. The mission never gets old. In fact, the more you feed it to people, the more you build your community of advocates that go out and work on your behalf to bring more customers into your orbit.

This means that your job is really to get out there with your potential customers and have conversations, whilst bringing them along on the journey. Always showcase the journey, your message in action. This is not you pushing features and functions but the broader essence of what it is you do and why you are doing it. It highlights where you are going, the problems you solve, and the pain you relieve for your specific type of customer. When this set of potential customers falls in love with what your business stands for, with its values, then they will lean in.

This is the tipping point of the first domino. This is when it wobbles, teeters and falls over, knocking over the next domino in the line. This is where everything changes, and it's the exact point you want to be out in the market selling to your next customer. And you guessed it, that's not by saying "please buy my product...", it's by having conversations and finding out how you are uniquely positioned to help your customer and provide greater customer value. When you get this, and it's timed with the fall of your first domino, it will create a ripple effect. You'll go from win to win to win. It will happen quickly and everywhere all at once, the floodgates will open, and you'll be there to receive it all.

The first domino is a huge moment, and you should celebrate it with everything you've got; celebrate it, commemorate it, do something special and do something different for your customers. Your customers want to see your business out in the wild, they want to see others using it, they want to hear about the wins from the perspective of the user.

You are in the business of what your business creates. You are not in the business of selling products, so sell the outcome, sell the broader message, be all about that and all in. That way you can create a brand and reputation for that industry and that's what spreads. Products are a dime a dozen, but a founder that is relentlessly going after it, pushing a bigger message than his or her company and product, is one that will attract all the attention.

Get creative and get wild. You want to make this bigger than you, bigger than your current company. You've got to get creative with how you spread your message. Your message is timeless; it's a legacy, so therefore you should be doing something special with it. Creating moments that you'll look back on and say, "We did it. We did something special. We took it to the next level. We weren't like everyone else. We made an impact."

Here's the rub: you've got to be ALL IN, with magnetic energy. Most people get the all-in part. They'll say, "Tim, I'll do whatever it takes. This is my life, and I want this to work." It has to work, but the problem is that they will never let go of the roller coaster. Their emotions are tied up in the external results of the business, so they go from being on top of the world one day to being in literal hell the next.

Instead, you've got to get that magnetic energy. It comes from

CHAPTER 6: QUESTION EVERYTHING

within. The way you determine success comes from within. You are beaming so brightly because you aren't attached to the outcome. Inside, you are already winning, you are doing your best in every moment and, because you are having deep conversations, asking big questions and living in this world of possibility, where good things keep happening, you're creating magic, from the inside out.

The world and our current results are just a reflection of our inner world. Life is a mirror, and we see what we think about. We either see all of the connections and synchronicities or we miss them completely because we are too close, holding on too tightly, in a state of fear and anxiety. We are letting negativity run the show.

Have you ever had a bad boss? And by *bad* I mean someone who was anxiety ridden, allowing fear to run the show. It sucks. But what's really going on in those cases? Is it their ability causing them to fail? Their lack of experience? Or just a succession of poor decisions?

No, what makes the anxiety-ridden leader bad is that they're not willing to face the truth and, because of that, they take everyone on this rollercoaster of emotions, charging in one direction on one day and then the opposite direction the next. You can't create to your fullest ability from a place of fear. Fear is a great motivator, but it will only get you so far. Then you are just placing all your bets on hope, wishing, and trying to make it work.

This type of leader is stuck because they make the external result linked to their self-worth. If they can't make the sale or hit their revenue goals then it means they are a terrible salesperson. Rather than being the entrepreneur that can say they learnt from their experiences, their losses and then got better, this type of leader takes the hit as a personal failure of capability. When they lead like this, nothing will ever be enough, past results don't mean shit, and the whole organisation becomes tilted towards external validation.

When you live for external validation, especially in a startup that hasn't made many sales, it crushes the momentum. Like a cloud of darkness, it shrouds the way and, instead of making the connections and following the steps, they shoot blindly in the dark, hoping to score. The other issue is, with all this dark energy going around, they are susceptible to lying, not owning their truth, taking shortcuts to win deals, over-pricing, over-extending, over-promising, and not being capable of empathy and long-term business relationships. It clouds their judgement and it makes it hard for trust to be built internally and externally with teammates and clients, but also with themselves. It's the exact opposite of magnetic; it's flat, dead, dull, muted, stunted, misplaced and diseased.

However, success, true success, comes as easily as the day follows night. It's effortless in the sense that you don't have to force it. You have to do your part, training your skills, your attitude, your mindset, and your question asking ability so that they flow at the right time and in the right way. You need to have faith and know that with every step forward you are a step closer to gold. You need to understand how to inspire others along the way, giving out what you want to receive.

In the spirit of this chapter, I want you to question everything, so I want you to start by questioning how you are showing up.

- Are you light energy when you are with potential clients?
- How do you react when a sale doesn't go your way? Or when a teammate needs help?
- Are you judging them, others in your industry or company?
- Do you make time for other people?
- Are you always in a rush to prove you're the best?
- Where do you find real joy in your life?
- What's lighting you up right now, getting that fire inside you roaring?
- What do you need to let go of?

CHAPTER 6: QUESTION EVERYTHING

- Where are you blocking your own desires and limiting yourself?
- What conversations do you need to be having that you aren't? Which customers are you avoiding?
- What information are you missing that would be helpful to know? What question do you need to ask to help you to uncover this information?
- Where are you out of alignment with your clients?
- What specific details do you wish you confirmed with your clients in your meetings?
- What are your intentions for every day?
- Where are you placing most value in the sales process?
- Are you all in on the process of the sales journey?
- What keeps you up at night about your business? What's the real fear you are hiding?
- Are you doing what you say you will do?
- What are you hiding?
- Where do you need to improve?
- Is your self-worth attached to the external result?

These questions will help to guide you towards some things you'll need to contemplate. Set some time aside to get clear on these and take the right actions today.

THE FIRST DOMINO

TODAY'S DOMINO CHALLENGE

I want you to use this 10-step formula for question asking in your next five meetings. The reason needs no explanation.

Question type	Why?	
Broad open-ended	To uncover	
Specific Aspirational	Probe for areas to help	
Specific Detrimental	To create urgency and push change	
Criteria and impact	To uncover	
Future oriented	Inspire and gather information	
Targeted insight	Gain understanding (must be a curious tone when asking)	
Diagnostic questions	Get specifics	
Conversation continuation	Keep them sharing	
Filler statements	Create ease, flow and excitement	
Alignment	Get buy in	

CHAPTER 6: QUESTION EVERYTHING

Question	Completed (Tick)
What's going on with you these days?	
What kinds of opportunities do you see for improvements in this area?	
What's holding you back from reaching your goals?	
How do you think the executive team or the board will evaluate the success of this project?	
Imagine it's three years from now. We're celebrating a successful partnership. What would have to happen to make that so?	
Why is this your strategy? Why do you see that working?	
Do you think (X) is a problem for you?	
Tell me, go on, how so?	
You're kidding, now I'm intrigued.	
This is what we discussed and here are the next steps, am I missing anything?	

CHAPTER 7
ADOPT THE MINDSET

I NEED you to be loose, relaxed, owning your journey, OK with failure, inspired by your attempts and your ability to try your best, so that you can get back up, dust yourself off and keep going. That needs to be your fuel. The way you get up every morning is "today's a new day to go create, to go give it my best shot and, if I do that, I am winning. I am here for all of it, not just the finish line. I am all in, and willing to go the distance."

    I help others to achieve their goals. I am an introduction-making machine. I am a connector, and I bring people together. I make things happen. I don't judge my success by how many deals we sign. I judge it by how many times I am willing to get rejected and carry on regardless. I know my truth and have value to offer. I don't look outside for external encouragement; I fuel it and stoke the flames of passion in the knowledge that I was born to do this. I was put here on this planet to bring this business into the world, and this is my destiny.

    I show up with a smile on my face, a song in my heart and an air of gratitude wherever I go. I am deeply connected to the source. I feel grateful that I get to do this as it's a privilege to have the opportunity. No matter the client's reaction, the unhelpful people I encounter, the rain and the wind, I am grateful to be here, and I am going to show up today. I will see the good in all things and know that I am being guided towards my fullest potential. Every day is a day to improve, to hone my craft, to learn about my customer. Every day is a day to win hearts and minds and plant more seeds to harvest in the summer.

I am on a mission and will infuse this with everyone I meet. I am always in launch mode. I won't stop because we have reached the finish line. Instead, I'll keep on running past the touchdown line and out of the stadium because I am locked in, so focused on making it happen.

I say all this because sometimes we all need a pep talk. We might get off track or find ourselves stuck in a rut, but now it's time to be honest, to take stock of where we are and answer those questions with real integrity.

I'll share a story. I got made redundant once. After receiving the news, the first thing I did was drop to my knees and ask for God's protection and guidance for my family. I asked for him to guide my path. I made it my mission to secure a job quickly and without panic. I locked in.

I knew it was a mindset game. I never once talked about it as a "job loss" or "redundancy", instead I called it a transition. I tuned my mind into the fact that I was transitioning jobs, as if it was planned, needed and all working out in my favour. I never imagined or gave energy to what would happen if I couldn't find a job in six months or a year, or what it would cost me to keep funding my lifestyle, what it would cost me in the way of missed investment opportunities or time. I only focused on what I could create in the now. I slowed down time. I made each day count. I mean, I really slowed down time. I got more out of a week than I had ever done. Not in a frantic way, in a strategic way. I only applied to jobs that I could see myself doing. It was a quality over quantity approach.

I prepared well for every conversation. I hit the gym an hour before each interview and came in light and free. I was unattached. The moment my mind would flick to "you need to land this role, Tim", I'd quickly think of the fact that this was a transition and that I didn't need it really. I wouldn't give that energy, energy. I didn't feed it. I gave that thought no oxygen, no room to catch fire. My mindset was focused only on creating opportunities, inspiring others with my interest in their business and what I saw in them. I was liberating myself from the idea that I needed to get a job and flipped it so that it was me interviewing them. I no longer needed it. Instead, I was selecting my next place of work.

The energy dynamic was how it was supposed to be because I valued what I could bring to the table. I valued myself. The situation wasn't going to guide the outcome, *I* was. My mindset was rock solid. Within a week of deciding, I had multiple balls up in the air. This gave me a chance to practise, to refine my pitch, to own my story, to get into my groove answering questions. It was a blessing. Every interview became an opportunity to meet someone new, find out about their business, as well as test what worked and what didn't. Each interview was a mini-experiment, taking me closer to the goal.

It was written. I knew I would secure a new role fast. There was never a doubt in my mind. Even in a situation where the pressure could make you need it too much, doubt that it was going to happen and get caught up in the story that everyone wanted you to hear. People would respond with "that sucks", or "I am so sorry", or "that's awful". I stopped telling people. It wasn't helpful. I controlled who I let into my circle. I didn't speak about "what if" or any bad outcomes. I didn't spend time with anyone who wanted to tell me how bad the job market was. I controlled the narrative and what I fed my brain. Each day was a mini-week.

Once we got moving, it created momentum and more roles came to me. I inspired companies to make a role where there was none, to move roles to my country, to connect with me. The dynamic was right. I was in flow and making it happen. I had guidance and was protected. My mind was at one with the outcome I wanted to create.

I tell you this story because it's the same for you and your business and landing that first big client. You must control what you feed your mind. Don't let others' expectations become your truth. If you say, "I will have my first client within 90 days", then get clear on channelling all your thoughts, all your energy and start to push deeper into that world.

Shut out anything or anyone who can't get onboard with this, who wants to tell you that it won't happen. Don't read the news, don't feed anything that isn't this outcome happening. Get some balls up in the air. Be OK with testing out your pitch. Go for quality over quantity, focus only on opportunities you'd be excited to work on. Master your energy. Mix it up, loosen up. Hit the gym two hours before a big pitch. Rock into your office 30 minutes before the call and know that you are meant to be here. This is a transition to your next client. This is not the big leap you are making it out to be. It's purely a transition. It's already happened in your mind.

Get to know the prospect with genuine curiosity. Be real, be authentic, be you in all your glory. It's you interviewing them. Do you want to do business with them? You're a busy entrepreneur, and you've got things going on. You came to play but you want to make sure you're spending your time on worthwhile projects.

When you do this, you become laser focused, allowing you to see what's not for you. You trust your intuition, so you don't chase, instead you attract. It's a big shift in your thinking and what you allow in. You control your mental world and the thoughts you allow. You say "no" a lot more. You don't share everything with everyone. You prepare, you deliver. You have value to offer.

Armed with this mindset, you're ready to do business. This is where you take it to the next level. You master your presentation, you perfect the script, you have flow with the words because you are confident; the more you practise, the more you master delivery and timing.

Every presentation needs an agenda. This is because you want people to know where they are going so that they won't interrupt you, or jump to the end before you've begun, because you are creating a moment. This presentation is an experience. You are going to bring it home, your confidence is apparent and in that feeling the client can relax into being guided by you as the expert.

Because you aren't trying to "sell to them", the buds of trust start to form and here's where you can take control of the conversation. You are only there to do what's right for your client. You are in that room, doing your thing, and the only reason you are there is to help them to do the right thing, whatever that may be. This is what differentiates you from all the other sharks out there. You only want this outcome. If they aren't the right client for your business, you're fine with that, but let's make sure we get to that outcome for the right reasons. You are their trusted advisor and that means doing the right thing for them. Can you see where I am going with this?

The presentation needs to conclude with what you have told them tailored for what they have told you. You need to weave in what they have offered as their reasons for doing business. When you get that right, you create a moment. It's why you need to be present, focused on them and their outcomes and not yours.

When you are using their needs, the things that they have outlined that are important to them, then you get buy in. Because you are an advisor and will do the right thing, you'll be able to make the assessment correctly that either you've got what they need or you don't. If you don't, be abundant enough to walk away, rather than trying to make your product fit.

At any point during the conversation, you should know this: the person asking the questions has the power. If you are faced with an objection, don't get hostile. I understand what it's like: this business is your baby and it's like someone just called your child ugly to your face. It's confronting but, rather than take offence, here's what I need you to do.

Ask a question.

This is going to give you way more insight into where they are at and, more valuably, what they are comparing you to. What they say next is gold, so you need to listen, really listen. Stop thinking about your ugly baby and pay attention.

Here's where you find out what you need to know so that you can figure out how to actually help them. This is where they tell you what they know or have been told by your competitors. Here's where they share their position and why. It gives you an opportunity. That is all an objection is, it's a massive opportunity to either set the record straight, build interest, share insight, expand knowledge or work together. It's actually the exact opposite to what most people see it as. Therefore, I need you to change how you perceive and hear objections. I need you to see them as opportunities, positive ones.

A client without objections is not a good client. The one with objections can actually be closer than you think to working with you, if you get it right. This means not reacting emotionally, and instead actually agreeing with their objection.

I studied psychology at university. It has been a big passion of mine to develop my understanding of human behaviour. I thought I would go on to get a PhD in it, and I may still do at some point, but for right now I found that business gifts you a front-row seat to real life. So, think of it like this: with objections you can either arc up and push back, creating conflict and little chance to understand and gather more information, or alternatively, you can agree with the objection and neutralise it. It takes the power out of the punch, removes the friction and the sting from it. That is what you want.

If they say "your pricing is too expensive", you should say "I agree: we are premium, I get it. We are the most expensive on the

CHAPTER 7: ADOPT THE MINDSET

market. Here's why. In order to have the highest quality checks we do XYZ..."

The agreement gives you the platform to have a conversation. To probe deeper.

Another strategy for this same objection is to say, "Can I ask why you think this?" Then you can leave it there... in silence. They will then explain who they are comparing you to, reveal more details as to competitor pricing and give you the information you need to help them.

When you are working to help them do the right thing, it's easy. When this is your motivation, when you don't want to do business that's not right, you are relaxed and neutral. You aren't even phased by this objection.

The cool thing is, when you get so good at this, you expect the objection, and because you hear it so frequently it doesn't phase you. You aren't frustrated because you see it as an opportunity to get to know where they are at and why. You probe deeper and you know that this is your chance to create a moment. Handle this well, uncover the details and show them how and why you are set up the way you are, and you'll make magic.

This is where the action really happens, but your success rests in how you handle this moment. It is in the words you say, how you say them, or even what you don't say. How you remove the tension in the room, lowering the emotional temperature, and then unpack the objection will dictate the result of the meeting. See it for what it really is: an opportunity to get closer.

Learning how to sell is the best skill you can develop today. You are 100% on the right track by picking up this book and investing in yourself.

It's about service mindset, changing your filter so you can see opportunities to help and communicate that desire to support others in a way that really lands.

Right now, how well developed this skill is for you will dictate how your results are doing in the way of revenue.

This is where self-awareness comes in. The opportunities are all around you, except you don't see them because you are only looking at the world through your current level of awareness.

However, the more you practise the tactics in this book, the more you'll develop social aptitude. You'll see how to deal with people, convincing people and being confident in your value whilst having certainty around exactly when you can help. It's the conviction that creates the opportunity to explore; you can ask better questions, when you aren't attached to losing the opportunity. You can probe deeper and with more curiosity.

If you're leading a team, they are watching how you show up and analysing your level of emotional maturity when things don't go as planned. This is also part of the mindset of a top sales leader. If you are charging into meetings, not navigating objections with grace, not understanding how to build people up and unable to control your emotional energy, then you will lose talent and sales opportunities.

Master emotional maturity so you can lead; it starts with you. When things go wrong in a meeting, or a potential client shows resistance to your product or idea, try not to be triggered. Stop your emotional reaction in its tracks, otherwise you are slipping into self-sabotage. When you are able to separate yourself from the outcome so that you don't flip the lid, this is where you can go to the next level and see it for what it is.

Most unskilled salespeople lose the sale at this point. Acting unprofessionally, huffing and puffing when clients don't agree with them or challenge their product. It can happen at all levels; this is not just a rookie mistake. I've seen MDs, CEOs, CFOs all lose their cool in front of clients, and this is a sure fire way to stop any business from expanding.

Your team are watching, they see how you react, and the real guns in business want nothing to do with a hot-head.

Top salespeople want a composed leader who has the emotional maturity to help guide their clients through the situation, despite their lack of understanding, scepticism or initial push back.

Managing your emotions is by far one of the best ways to help you to attract talent. I've seen founders create fantastic businesses then want to hire top talent to expand into new markets, yet the only reluctance in the talent's mind is: can I work for you with your attitude and the way you operate?

If you have control of yourself, stop reacting and live with self-awareness, then talent will come to you, but only when they see you leading yourself.

Make emotional regulation your superpower. Detach from the outcome. Detach from the meaning, change what it means when a client objects or decides not to move forward. True abundance is not attached to outcome. It's plentiful.

Sales is a skill that once developed will unlock more than just the door to riches. It's about developing your mindset. You must be hyper intentional about the words you speak. It's about knowing deep down within yourself that you will make it happen, that you will see your dream come into reality. You must have that conviction.

The truth is that the majority of salespeople are mediocre; you just have to look at the numbers because the data will tell you. If you want to breathe that rare air as a top sales professional, all you must do is focus on developing yourself, your skill, your ability to take action when everyone around you doesn't believe or is discouraging. You must proceed and progress despite the challenges, obstacles and adversity. It's like anything else: it happens in the face of the doubters. A tree grows strong roots because of the storm, the plane takes off flying into the wind, this is what creates lift, having something to push against. Testing your mettle is actually a good thing as it sharpens you and says, "how badly do you want this? What are you willing to do? Who are you willing to become to get it?" The possibility that it can happen is always there, that's what scares most people. It's the realisation that they are the problem, and they need to get better, not that the situation is too hard.

If you've ever heard of Price's Law, which states that 50% of the production comes from the square root of that domain, then it probably sounds complicated – but it's not. It means if you produce $100,000 as a business, 50% (so $50,000) is produced by the square route of 100, which is 10. Simply put, 10% of your salespeople bring in 50% of your revenue. Or another example is, 10% of your accounts provide 50% of your profits. The thing to note here, and the point I am making, is that the further you go up the easier it is to produce more.

Therefore, when you become the best in your industry at what you do, you get access to more sales, more high-quality opportunities and more overall success than the rest because you attract this good fortune.

By becoming a top tier salesperson – the best that you can be, focusing on your craft, working on your communication skills, like your tone, pace and delivery, working on your humor and ability to make people feel at ease and bringing people together – your success at being a connector is all that counts.

Eliminate words like "I'll try", instead say "I will", forget "I think", "I hope", "I should", and instead replace them with "I am", "I can", "I do". Summon that conviction. Stand tall.

We want certainty, definiteness, and intention with our words – it is paramount. We must train our subconscious to see the world we want, so our dreams are realised. The idea and the person always become ready before the money arrives. Definiteness of purpose is one of those characteristics when you can tell it's on the way.

Talking of money, how do you feel about it? Do you see it as

CHAPTER 7: ADOPT THE MINDSET

abundant, in infinite supply, everywhere, as a tool to do more of what you love and produce, a thing to be multiplied and made more of? Or do your feelings towards money lean towards its lack, never having enough, stress, strife and struggle, wishing and hoping?

Money is there to help you make more of it. Plain and simple. It's everywhere and will come more abundantly and quickly into your life when you are not chasing it, when you don't seek it in desperation, but attract it by becoming better, by moving in a direction, in a certain way, with boldness, decisiveness and swagger. It wants you if you behave this way around it. Nothing can stop the person who believes fully that they can get what they want and takes the actions required to get it.

Your approaches to money and sales go hand in hand; if you want sales to be effortless then focus on getting better, on self-development, on refining your skills, and on finding a mentor, someone in the field of sales that you admire, and then start to copy them. You need to think like them, you need to see money as an easy thing to acquire and you need to start making your big goals smaller. For example, with the first domino, the only reason it's not happening is because you've made it this big deal in your mind, when we release that, and switch our mindset to it being just the first step of many on the journey to freedom, when we see the first big client as small and expected, it changes how we show up. Our whole physiology changes, and energetically we shift.

We can engage with the client instead of trying to sell to them because we are not trying to land them desperately out of fear. We aren't focusing on the fact that we won't be able to pay the bills as an entrepreneur or that we'll face judgement if they don't sign amidst the pressure of our quarterly target.

I get it. As an entrepreneur, founder, CEO of a business, your full focus and attention is on generating cashflow as quickly as humanly possible, so you can raise more money and expand.

As a sales professional, you want some semblance of job security, and the best way you can think to establish that is by hitting targets, winning a flurry of flagship clients and making ridiculous amounts of hay whilst the sun shines.

Either way, you're ambitious and hungry to move up the ranks asap with lucrative promotions. You want to earn much more through accelerators, experience President's Clubs and have an epic life! I get it.

But the pressure of this dominating your mindset is impacting upon how you show up in front of the very people you need to be unattached from.

When this is your driving force (the negative of what might happen if they don't sign), then it limits the situation and puts a cap on what you can do.

When you come from a place of service, and a mindset of abundance, understanding and adventure, and you practice the sales skills to become great, then it liberates you.

The meaning you place on events has a big effect on how you perceive what is going on in your life.

High energy and low energy.

A quick rule of life. Get away from energy vampires (as Jon Gordon calls them in *The Energy Bus*, great book!) and get with the energy elevators. People that light up a room, inspire and talk about possibilities at every moment. Wealthy people just have a greater awareness of how money works and what's possible. They are wealthy in mind because of how they see the world not because of the wealth they have acquired. How they see situations, and what's possible, allows them to overcome more obstacles, connect the dots and keep moving forward, with an attitude of gratitude, even when it looks like everything is going wrong.

They aren't limited by circumstance because they have overcome circumstance when times were hard. They became the

CHAPTER 7: ADOPT THE MINDSET

person they needed to be based on their goals and then took this action, despite the adversity and hard situations.

This means they faced the rejection. The times that their client wouldn't meet them, and they carried on regardless, they knew that if they just kept going, and pushed to get to that rare air, and became the best in the industry at what they did, success would eventually find them.

When the rejection comes and the client turns down your proposal, don't be disheartened, don't stop doing the work, in fact use it as fuel. Know that you are on the right track, take the lessons and iterate and keep moving forward.

"You don't get to pick and choose when to show up, because the world will ignore your best and judge you for your worst.

"If you want to win, your responsibility is to show up with the energy and enthusiasm for the little things just as much as you do for the big things."

– SAHIL BLOOM

A question I encourage you to ask daily to inspire more possibility, as referenced by Frederik Pferdt in the book *What's Next Is Now*, is, "What would need to happen for this to be true?" In playing with this question regularly, it stimulates an open dialogue that is inquisitive and investigative and helps you to form the habit. By probing the edges and questioning in this manner your imagination can go to work and, through this process, new options reveal themselves.

TODAY'S DOMINO CHALLENGE

This one's a biggie. There are three areas to focus on.

- Do an audit of your circle: who's draining your energy? What conversations shouldn't you be having? Identify them and remove yourself from them, change the subject or say you have to make a call and leave. Energy vampires are keeping you stuck, planting ideas that have no merit in your mind. The quicker we remove these negative nellies from your daily intake of content the better.

    As Patches O'Houlihan said in the movie *Dodgeball*, "If you're going to become true dodgeballers, then you've got to learn the five d's of dodgeball: dodge, duck, dip, dive and dodge!"

    Same for you and complaining, moaning, takers in life. Do everything in your power to limit your presence with these people. Takers are the worst, it's easy to spot them. They are nice as pie until they get flustered, or thrown off guard, and then they reveal their true intentions and manipulative nature.

- Where do you need to get more emotional control? Dial in on this aspect of how you show up.

    Are you too hot-headed? Where are you reacting rather than being neutral? What situations do you quickly need to become much better at handling?

- I want you to become obsessive about being intentional with your words this week. For 7 days, take inventory of yourself, correct yourself when you use weak uncommitted words ("I'll try") or poor language to describe a situation.

CHAPTER 7: ADOPT THE MINDSET

> Do you use bad language obsessively? Is it really shit? Really? Or could you take ownership and be better? Was it their fault? Or could you have prepared more, changed the situation? These minor tweaks make the largest difference. It all counts. Internally to your subconscious and externally to your clients. Everything matters. Now, it's time to level up!

CHAPTER 8
REMEMBER LOVE

I HOPE you can start to see that you are the secret sauce that brings everything to life. Your enthusiasm, passion and dedication, combined with your desire to work for your clients' greater good, is what influences others and moves mountains.

Your love for the process, for your clients' positive business outcomes, is what sees you accelerate. It's your commitment to refining your presentation. This is what we talk about when we say "doing the work"; it's perceived as boring but actually this is where you align the stars. You find that magic sentence, that way of phrasing things that is actually you – it's your secret sauce. This is an energy; it unlocks doors.

This is why you need to be very conscious of the people, thought processes and mindsets you are allowing into your life. Think about your family; they love you, but when they give you advice it comes from their own experiences. So how can they give you advice if you are attempting to do things that they haven't done? It doesn't make sense. They are saying these things because they don't want to see you hurt or in pain. They are trying to help you the best way they know how, but they don't have the perspective or experience to comment on what you are doing. It makes no sense. This can go for managers, stakeholders, business partners, spouses; you've got to be careful who you let into your mind as a perspective to consider. Everyone's just giving you their take but selling it like they've done what you are trying to do.

The other more distracting part that can cause you to go off track is others who see your magnetism, momentum and energy and want a piece of it for themselves. They will want your attention because they are looking to create it for themselves. Whilst being a mentor or helping out a friend is noble; it won't help you build your business beyond a certain point. Teaching others is a brilliant way to solidify your own thinking, but watch out for those people that want to talk to you for hours. They are slowing you down, derailing you, keeping you treading water.

You need to be locked in, daily, allowing consistency to build. You need to go off the grid for a bit from these people and push deeper into your client conversations. Be inaccessible. I know it feels good to be wanted but we need to limit access for right now. You are focused on producing some outcomes that change the game for your life, therefore we need you in creation mode, being the lighthouse for your clients and leading the way.

Illuminate the path for others through your example, not through your time. Or cap it and make sure you stick to it. Set up a weekly hour meeting to have these conversations and be intentional with your time. I need you to gain some control over this as it will run away with you if you let it. The productive person doesn't have time to be all things to all people – they are intentional with their time. They kick goals because they prioritise goal kicking activities.

You are so powerful. You have within you a force that brings things to reality. Use that energy for good. Bring people together. Don't hold back. Limit time spent around nervous energy vampires and people that make you feel drained.

When you love the process, you're not feeling down because you got a "no" or that proof of concept didn't progress. You've got enough balls in the air that you're going to bring them in, one after another. It's inevitable. Your conviction and confidence will

CHAPTER 8: REMEMBER LOVE

inspire progress. It's all created internally first, before you bring it to life through action.

See this inevitability in your mind. Love your clients in your mind and feel gratitude for them. Exist in this space. People will say you got lucky. Let them. They don't know the formula and, while they waste their time taking shortcuts, comparing score cards, wishing and hoping for something to stick, you'll be making a foundation you can build upon.

Jim Rohn said, "Success isn't something you pursue, it's something you attract." And he was right!

In his 2024 commencement speech to Dartmouth College, Roger Federer said, "In tennis, perfection is impossible. In the 1,526 singles matches I played in my career, I won almost 80% of those matches. Now, I have a question for you, what percentage of points do you think I won in those matches? Only 54%. In other words, even top ranked tennis players win barely more than half of the points they play. When you lose every second point on average you learn not to dwell on a shot."

The lesson here is that you must lock onto the sale that's in front of you now. When you are in a meeting or an interaction, lock onto that specific interaction even if adversity happened just minutes prior. Don't focus on the lost sale moments before, don't carry the weight of a disagreement yesterday into today. Each day, each moment becomes an opportunity to start with every intention to add value to the clients you are with. When you are going from meeting-to-meeting, back-to-back-to-back, which tends to happen when you are flying into a market for a few days and want to have as many needle moving conversations as possible, this is where you need to lock in.

Dial in your focus so the person you are with becomes the most important thing in the world. It has to be. This is the energy transfer, the opportunity to influence, and your mindset can't dwell on the last meeting, the negativity of the taxi driver that got you to the client's office, the pessimism of the last customer you saw. All of it has to be and stay behind you. You can only be free if you let it go.

This is the skill you are really training. Not carrying the emotions into meeting after meeting and turning one dead end into a series of dead ends. You need to be able to carry on with all the energy, purpose and presence of an entrepreneur on a mission to serve. Believe in your mind that this is where you are meant to be. See your words flow, so stop holding the tension in your neck, and let it go. Enjoy the process. Be in this moment.

Most people aren't thinking big enough and it's the same for your clients, so don't let this pattern shrink your vision. If anything, you should go bigger; there's less competition for those who think bigger.

If you want to become a master at sales, you need to be able to accept that you will lose ten times and win once, and you can deal with that ratio happily. It doesn't affect your mindset, or your drive. It's the attitude you have towards loss that makes you win. When you can keep going with the same enthusiasm and clarity, putting your all into what you do, to refine your presentation, to get so good at delivering your story that you can do it anywhere anytime and make it look effortless. It's this perpetual experimentation and commitment to refinement that speaks volumes.

This is the winning combination, the place that most don't master, and the difference is vast. Stop giving power to your problems. Those who can block out the negativity and wasted energy and redirect it into goal achieving activities and deliberate action are the ones that go on to produce and multiply in the greatest quantities.

There's something poetic about sales. When you fall in love with service mindedness, and a willingness to leave everyone better off than the time you found them, then you win at life.

CHAPTER 8: REMEMBER LOVE

Winning at life is the ultimate success. It's a lifestyle win, living life on your terms. It's not the accolades and the money, it's the freedom and what you can do with it that counts - the experiences, memories and the adventures. The good life. Remember that there is no dress rehearsal when it comes to life. When you are so dedicated to your craft that you are determined to become the best in the world at what you do and continue to work towards that goal, that's something rather special.

As you progress, and especially in the attraction of success, you'll be opening doors that are bigger than you think you can handle. You'll be surprised. When you start to move with intention and you expect good things to happen, things move into place, sometimes faster than you are prepared for. So, the aim of the game is to be prepared. Always be ready. That's why working on yourself every day is magic.

You may be invited to do a panel, to share your expertise, your story and lessons with the industry. You should one hundred percent say "yes" to this opportunity. It will be a valuable experience and the people you'll meet along the way will be game changing. Often those also on the panel with you will form a special bond, as you've been through something together; you've created an experience and cultivated a compelling argument for your cause. It's transformational and enjoyable.

How to conduct yourself at a conference you are speaking at. Try not to get overly stressed if it's your first time doing something of this nature. You'll naturally feel uneasy because it matters to you and also because it is unknown. Don't worry: everyone, no matter how many times they have done it, feels like this right before they go on stage. Even if they are the CEO.

Here are a few bullet points to guide you through this and turn it into an area to excel in:

- Be mindful of the types of conversations and people you are around in the one hour prior to your panel; thoughts are contagious.
- When you get on the stage, smile. It's super easy to forget to smile because you are focused, blinded by the bright lights on stage, and you don't want to trip up because you are worried about all the faces in the crowd. Just relax and remember that you are on the big screen and your expression is sending a message, so smile. Even if you don't feel like it inside. Smiling has a powerful effect.
- Power-pose right before you get up there. It will boost your confidence and help you to feel stronger and bolder.
- Know that you are filled with light and love. It's not about you, it's about serving others.
- Have your points to each of the questions written out on cards. Don't use them, just keep them in your pocket.
- Be yourself, don't try to copy anyone else. Instead, just relax into you and love yourself. This is very much about self-acceptance.
- Kill any doubt the moment it arises. Use your mindset to think about the situation you want to happen, not what you don't.
- Take your time, don't rush. If your mind goes blank, remember to take a breath. This will help you to refocus instead of starving your brain of oxygen.
- Have fun, try to establish rapport with the other panellists 30 minutes prior to the panel.
- Tell stories. They are more memorable for both you and the audience and they are expressive too. Draw out the emotion of each story as it will help the audience to connect to you.
- Don't be afraid to improvise and be spontaneous. If a valuable idea comes up, go with it.

CHAPTER 8: REMEMBER LOVE

- Practise beforehand but don't be wedded to your script. Know where you are going to take the audience directionally and then take them there.
- Don't believe anyone who tells you they haven't done any preparation or can't remember what they are going to say. They have and they will.
- If the seat they give you is an uncomfortable stool and not a proper chair, for the guys, remember to close your legs more than normal. Sitting with one foot on the floor and one resting on the stool rung is a way to look casual and professional.

This is a bigger version of you that you are stepping into and it's a great one. This will generate leads, spark interest, set you up as an expert in your field and put you light years ahead of anyone else looking to compete. When you evangelise what you are doing for the benefit of others, it's a positive shift up. Remember, this is not about you, it's about sharing valuable insights and bringing people on the journey. Connect to their hearts. Give them a good show. Let them get to know you and you'll be surprised how much you enjoy it.

When you start doing panels, you can leverage them to scale your outreach. They take less preparation than putting on an event yourself and you can hit a larger group of people en mass. Don't underestimate the power of awareness and association. Once you've done a few of these, you'll be a dab hand at your preparation. You'll feel more at ease and then you'll really hit your stride.

It's the same with the press and podcasts. You want to get as much attention as you can around your subject matter, so become seen as an expert and a go-to figure for a perspective. I remember when I started out as a writer and author that I would constantly send draft articles and pitches to publications to see if they wanted to explore working together. Nothing really took off. It wasn't until I won (i.e. book sales dramatically increased tenfold) that they cared. Now they are coming to me, requesting quotes for articles on the topic of negotiation. When you win, it all changes, everyone wants to hear about what you are doing. So what does that tell you? You must act as if you have already won. Only you need to cheer for you, so keep doing the needle-moving activities, taking the leap, acting as the person you want to become who already has achieved the thing you want to do. If you do that, then you'll get all the rest of the good stuff and more. Right after the reporters came the international rights and language translation deals. First Thailand, then Italy, then half of the South Asian countries.

What I am saying to you is, my friend, keep pushing. It all counts; even if you win by an inch, then you've taken new ground, increased your market share. You've won, and that win unlocks and attracts other big wins you couldn't even imagine occurring. When you take the action that a person who has done the thing you are looking to achieve would do, that's where it all changes.

The question is, what are you waiting for?

TODAY'S DOMINO CHALLENGE

Do some research on a few conferences and events that you could speak at, either on a panel or a guest speaker. It might seem annoying, but how badly do you want it? How far are you willing to go to make your dream a reality. The more you put yourself in the game, the more success will find you.

The spotlight is a great way to attract success because of the person you become by doing the work. A person who loves what they are doing is a person that takes the leap and says "yes" when an opportunity to maximise comes along.

CHAPTER 9
TELL THE STORY

You've got to take people on the journey, bring them along for the ride, share your thoughts. When you get exciting news about your business, post a video to LinkedIn that walks anyone who will listen through the steps it took to get there, the people you talked to, and your thinking on what's still to come.

Don't just post up a boring old text post and hope to stand out. Purposefully make a difference by being different. Every bit of news is an opportunity to share the story, to bring people with you, and to influence. This is how you create momentum, awareness and get buy-in.

They are buying into your purpose, what you stand for and the mission. Don't miss these golden opportunities to do that.

It's all about the story. The more you can make people feel like they know you and share openly, the more you can make a bigger impact. Be daring, post that video. Share more. How many people are doing that right now? Maybe 5%. All the rest are sheep, aimlessly posting, resharing and doing the same old thing but "hoping" to be an outlier, to go viral, to get more likes than the last post.

You've got to put yourself out there and take the risk; there is unlimited upside from making it a habit to take others on the journey. Don't over analyse or let fear stop you from posting it up. This is the exact thing you need to be doing much more of – making some noise; it might take 150 posts or it might take 500 before you get one that generates a lead, but this is what it takes to receive an outsized reward. If you keep showing up, and keep being real, there will come a point when you make success damn near automatic. You'll become a lead generation machine and, in the process of sharing willingly, you'll most certainly inspire and help more than a few people along the way.

The way to cut through is to be different, to rise above the noise and to be authentic, share stories, make it personal, give value through lessons and allow your audience (however small) to get to know you a bit better.

I'm not sure if it's because I am in the middle of writing this book, but I can't sleep past 2.30am right now. I wake up with these thoughts that I just need to share here. The next piece of the book is writing itself.

It happens every time, and it's become my process. It's been three nights in a row. The same applies to you; when passion grips you, absorb it, take advantage of it, grab a surfboard and ride that wave.

That's a good point. If a wave is coming, what options do you have? One, do nothing and get crushed by the wave; two, grab a board and learn to ride the wave; or three, invent a technology and transform that wave energy into something that can be captured, harnessed and used for good.

When you get in the flow, nothing and no one can stop you. You are converting the wave of momentum into energy that can propel your business forwards, but the main thing you should be doing when this hits is sharing the story. Talking to people, customers, anyone that knows something about the topic you are focused on. This is how you connect the dots, so get curious.

If you are looking to land a certain type of client, you need to get curious about the types of problems these clients have. Read books that solve the problems your clients have. Become an expert in them. The more ways you know to help them, the

CHAPTER 9: TELL THE STORY

more ways you'll be helpful. It could just be an introduction to a key relationship, the evolution of an idea, being a sounding board to bounce ideas off. As long as you're helping, you're progressing.

In fact, if you haven't already, I want you to post a video of why you started your business to LinkedIn right now. The purpose behind it. Where were you when you had the idea? What were you dealing with? How were you feeling? Why did you think it was needed? Where are you headed? Let people in. Share it up on LinkedIn and don't look back. Then go have a coffee with everyone who comments and likes the post. Spread the word. Get comfortable sharing more about your vision. You'll be surprised by the doors that open when you put it out there.

If you're not sure where to start with all this, I have a couple of questions for you.

Why are you doing this? What's the purpose of it? Is it to prove people who said you couldn't do it wrong?

I remember in maths class when Mr Godfrey told me I couldn't take the higher maths GCSE exam because the likelihood I would score below a D grade was high and below a D meant that I would have failed. This was enough to stir up a commitment to win, an enemy to battle, and it lit a fire in me. I told him to enter me for the higher paper. I went away, I did the work, I found the resources and, guess what, when you make a commitment to win, the right resources and people show up. They were always there, you just weren't the right person to see them; when your focus changes everything changes. When the student is ready, the teacher shows up. I took the exam and I got one of the highest grades in the class. I got an A.

Why did you start this business? Why are you in sales? Why did you take this job?

Is it to take your family to the next level and 50 levels above? Good! Now we're getting somewhere.

Is it bigger than that? Do you want to change your industry or some part of the world?

Once you have this nailed, you can dial in on what you're here to do. There's a seed inside of you that's been planted for you to express. The desire you have inside is there for a reason; the most alive we feel is when we are allowing the work to do its work on us, to bring out who we are supposed to become.

The reason it's tough is a great thing – it works on you, making you stronger, more resilient, more aware. Don't waste the journey and the multiplier effects it can have on you and your business because you fear what others will think. Just get into action mode and don't look back. Your story has the power to change the lives of people you haven't even met yet. When you come from this place and live in the spirit of this message, miraculous things happen, believe me.

The other thing to note is the story is always evolving: Lamborghini started off as a tractor company, Samsung used to be a grocery store, LG used to be a facial cream, Nokia's first product was toilet paper, Ikea started life as a pen. Everything is evolving all the time. This means your story can also evolve, grow and take shape as you develop. This is why taking your community on the journey with you is a continuous process. As you learn, they grow with you.

A butterfly starts life as a caterpillar, and it transforms; it goes into the darkness and, after a lot of struggling, emerges with beautiful wings and the ability to fly to new heights. Everything you are going through is preparing you for who you need to become to go where you want to go. Without the struggle you wouldn't gain the strength, awareness and transformation required to fly.

Telling the story also applies to when you are pitching a potential prospect. Your main job, as a salesperson, is to effectively communicate value, and you can do this through the power of

CHAPTER 9: TELL THE STORY

story. Research shows that stories are recalled 63% of the time, whereas stats are only recalled 5% of the time. That's an 11 times multiplier! Now we're talking! A couple of lines of well-articulated story, and we're off to the races. Not quite... the art of persuasion comes down to a multitude of other factors, such as the delivery, intonation and tone, the way you present certain information and allow it to build suspense. But more than this, persuasion is about heart. Someone can tell when you're all in, and you are doing it for the right reasons. They can also tell if you are downplaying the challenges and hurdles involved in the deal. They can spot if you are overselling it or being purposefully unclear. That's why a compelling story, presented with bold authenticity, vulnerability, and emotion can move mountains and build trust.

To highlight this point further, this is the story of Ben Francis, founder of Gym Shark. He's one of the youngest self-made billionaires ever. Ben went against the grain; he did something that other sporting brands had missed and, because of this, managed to build a $1.4 billion empire.

Back in 2012 Ben was studying at Aston University in Birmingham. He lived two lives very efficiently. He'd finish lectures around 4pm, then go directly to Pizza Hut to start his shift where he was either pot washing or out delivering pizzas until 10.30pm. His life was very functional, but it served a purpose: he had a massive amount of freedom, so, in between deliveries, he was consuming content on YouTube. When I say consuming, I mean every waking second in between his commitments Ben was devouring everything that a few gym influencers would upload. Ben was obsessed.

Ben realised there was nothing out there in the market like what he wanted to wear in the gym. He gave himself a test. Previously, he'd given himself small tests, like whether he could make an app, now he had to make a basic website that would transact. Next, he spent everything he had on a sewing machine and screen printer. Everything was custom made, leaving him to design the logos by hand; it was intense and manual.

Then he did something no one else in the space was doing. He changed the game! This was a pivotal moment for the fledgling startup. He decided to send the Gym Shark clothing to the fitness influencers he followed. Remember, back then no one else was doing influencer marketing as a competitive strategy to expand awareness. Ben recalls, when one of the athletes wore their product, it was "the coolest thing ever".

Instead of trying to compete with the monstrous marketing budgets of their behemoth competitors like Nike and Adidas, Ben took a different approach. He went direct to the source and looked at who was influencing the gym culture. This move came naturally to him. He recognised that fitness influencers had access to his customers. If he could collaborate with them, he could build trust.

This is a huge lesson for any startup: focus on going where your customers are. The question to ask is, who's got my customers? In the case of Gym Shark, their customers were all following these athletes in the gym who uploaded their workout content to YouTube. That meant, by getting the product into these influencers' hands, he could do something truly special. It was about precision and impact over gigantic advertising budgets.

These fitness influencers held the key to potential Gym Shark customers. For just $500 per influencer per month, Ben would send them free gear and they'd wear it in their videos, talk about it, and give feedback. Ben had tapped into something the big brands understood but were still searching to find, and that was trust. You don't buy trust from ad spend; trust comes through authentic connection and real feedback.

But the story doesn't end there. Ben took the biggest risk of his life with the company; he bet everything they had on one event.

CHAPTER 9: TELL THE STORY

Armed with the knowledge that fitness influencers were crucial to Gym Shark's current growth, he spent three hundred thousand pounds on a booth at Body Power, Europe's biggest bodybuilding expo.

It was a big bet, but in 2013 it mattered; he put it all on the line and the decision didn't come without its fair share of criticism. People thought he was insane.

But what happened next blew the doors wide open. It shocked the industry. They launched an exclusive product for the event that wasn't available online. They teased it on Facebook, then brought their heroes to the event, the very fitness influencers that had been repping their gear.

On the morning of the event, as Ben walked over to the stand, he saw a flood of people racing over to the Gym Shark booth. Hundreds of people were there to see Gym Shark. Sales exploded immediately: they went from $450 a day to $45,000 overnight. That's a 100x increase. Can you imagine expanding 100x in one day! Talk about the power of knowing your audience and having the conviction to take inspired action.

But the real genius wasn't just taking a crazy bet and it paying off 100-fold. Yes, that was awesome, but the magic happened behind the scenes. They were ready for this kind of expansion and success through the team that Ben had built. He had a 40-person data team whose sole purpose was to understand what gym goers wanted. The insights came from everywhere: Instagram engagement, fitness app usage, purchase history and workout habits. When Gym Shark launches a product, they work hard to make sure they have the best selection of data and they are buying exactly what the customer wants at the perfect time. This is what is at the heart of it.

This is the story of a guy who got obsessed and spotted an opportunity then willed it into existence. Can you imagine

THE FIRST DOMINO

deciding to set up a sports clothing brand to compete with Nike in 2012? Ben could. Ben's desire to be involved in the fitness community started with uploading supplements to the website and drop shipping them to customers, but recognising a need (that what the clothing customers wanted to wear wasn't available), he set about making it happen. Ben also did another thing that most entrepreneurs struggle with at a certain point: he recognised that he needed to get out of the way and focus only on what he was good at, allowing the rest of the team to focus on the areas in which they excelled.

Gym Shark has come a long way. By 2020, the fitness brand was valued at more than £1 billion. This happened because Ben understood the power of community building. Gym Shark focused on sharing their story, with content that mattered, like daily workout videos, training tips and success stories. Their YouTube channel went through the roof, their TikTok's got millions of views, and so they were no longer selling clothes, they were selling belonging and lifestyle.

This example is a representation of many of the strongest brands who achieve massive exponential growth seemingly overnight. These brands understand that you expand by sharing authentic stories and your journey. You build communities and share what's going on behind the scenes – every failure, every misstep, every win. It's all part of building trust and connection, and this is what translates to meaning and purpose. It's bigger than just the product you sell.

Side note, special thanks to Tim Carden's epic thread on X for this breakdown.

CHAPTER 9: TELL THE STORY

> ## TODAY'S DOMINO CHALLENGE
>
> I want you to go for a walk and then note down what comes to mind when you answer these questions outlined above. Keep going deeper, ask yourself "why?" seven times. It will help you pull back the layers and see what's driving you at your core.
>
> Next, I want you to post it up. Make sure that it conveys the emotion behind why you are doing what you do, offer a lesson or two to make it even more valuable and even add in a resource to help others. This could be a podcast episode you enjoyed, a mentor in the industry you look up to, or a few bullet points as tips to help others in the same boat.
>
> It matters. This is training you for the person you are going to become, someone who can throw posts up with ease, comment on others' content with effortlessness and flow, and bring the story to life.
>
> Being able to talk to the camera, write down your thoughts and compose a short story or two can now become a weekly event. You are ready, but the only person that can make it so is you.

CHAPTER 10
BECOME A MAGNET

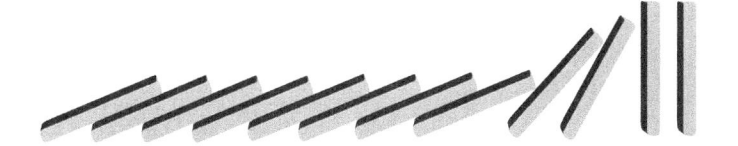

THE legendary Jim Rohn said, "Everything has four parts: one is cause, two is effect, three is direction and four is destination. The goals will become like a magnet – they will start to pull."

Remember this when you go about your day. You can become a magnet – everything is working for you, and in your favour, pulling you towards the bigger life you have targeted. At first it will seem alien, you're failing your way to success with missteps and learnings, but as you progress, you'll notice that you are climbing up the mountain, making significant advancements in areas you once were stagnant in or even avoiding.

Everything conspires in your favour. When you become magnetic, your intuition will speak more loudly and you'll begin to trust it. You will have conversations that drive you forward and elevate your thinking.

The next right step will appear, just as you need it, because you are becoming the person that can make that progress. You are walking the walk.

In this chapter I want to outline the big buckets so that, wherever you are headed, whatever business you are in, you will win at life and your goals. It might sound boring, but this is what works.

> "We resist new manoeuvres because they make us feel clumsy, awkward, and more at risk. But if you want to accelerate your rate of achievement rapidly, you must search out and vigorously employ new behaviours."
>
> **– PRICE PRITCHETT**

Becoming a magnet for success is the separator between "I nearly made it" and "it was inevitable". How can two people experience the same circumstance, yet achieve extraordinarily different outcomes? One goes on to build a multi-million-dollar empire and the other changes nothing. We have to learn to fear treading water.

It all comes down to this, are you ready? The ability to be able to live and embody the feeling of your goal as if it has already been achieved, exactly as you would feel it – no doubt, no worry, just pure acceptance that it has happened. All whilst continuously practising your daily processes. This is what makes you magnetic. It's not about resources, luck or timing, these things can be helpful, of course, but the real difference maker is who you've become inside. You can have all the resources in the world at your fingertips and still not create any magic, not reach your full potential, or achieve anything out of the ordinary. It's also true that you can have very little in the way of resources but, with the right processes practised daily in the spirit of faith, you can still transform.

Think back to Ben, the founder of Gym Shark we met earlier. He didn't have much to begin with externally, just a sewing machine, a printing press and the will to see his desire come

CHAPTER 10: BECOME A MAGNET

into reality. He believed it was possible and set about it with a magnetic energy.

This is what the elite salespeople do. It's their identity. When you have the identity of someone who's achieved big things, and really feel the emotion of it, you can go on to create something extraordinary and change people's lives.

Think about this as you read this next section. You have everything you need already, but you need to change how you are approaching your daily tasks, how you see the obstacles, and instead redefine them as an opportunity to grow. Nothing is in your path without good reason. It is forcing you to take responsibility for your part in it, to refine it and get better. This, my friend, is where your whole life is about to take off into a completely new realm of success.

One last thing: if you currently feel like you are just going through the motions, not excited about what you get to do, it is because of one thing and one thing only. You've forgotten your *why*, or you haven't spent the time to clearly define your why, and therefore it's hard to generate the automatic motivation needed to do the work. Your why needs to be crystal clear.

For those with a big enough why, action is automatic, they do it now. They don't procrastinate or hold back, they breathe possibility and life into situations, acting on their ideas in the moment. Have you forgotten your why? Take a moment to reflect on this now and get clear on exactly what it is you want. This needs to be a burning desire, an all-consuming obsession, something that deep within lights you up and ignites your commitment to have discipline in mindset.

This is not about forcing situations to change, or circumstances to be different, it's about having the courage, confidence and faith to trust that you are being guided, and that everything is working in your favour, because it is.

The real winners in life, those that are truly making it happen, have mastered the art of going with life's flow and trusting that everything is happening for the greater good. These magnetic individuals build quickly because they attract opportunities and circumstances into their lives and don't let the outside circumstances or results control them. They are completely neutral. Whether they succeed or fail, it's always a win. They take another step towards the realisation of their dream. It's all about how you see things. I need you to make a steadfast commitment to yourself that you'll do the following processes daily, that you'll keep this promise to yourself, because this will allow you to trust yourself deeply. This is what counts and where you become who you were always capable of being.

CAUSE

GO to bed at 9–9.30pm every night, get up at 4.30–5am every morning. It doesn't matter if you are on holiday, at a company offsite, or with friends on a ski trip, adhere to this rule and you will succeed in more ways than not. The consistency you bring to your sleeping pattern, the mischief, pain and laziness you will avoid by implementing this schedule will give you life. Exercise daily, whether this is lifting heavy weights, cycling, walking, boxing, yoga. You need to get out into the world and move.

Read daily, 10–20 pages. Read until you find something that lights you up and moves you mentally, spiritually, internally. The secrets to life are in the books you read. If you want to get ahead and be some place different a year from now, challenge yourself to read and make it a part of your daily habits. Practise gratitude for everything you have in your life right now and everything that is coming. Twenty pages a day is 35 books a year; the consistency and commitment to this one ritual develops a strong trust in yourself. It becomes part of your identity, of who you are. The daily feeling of accomplishment is a small victory which dramatically increases the velocity, conviction, and impact of your ideas.

EFFECT

BY sleeping when others don't, you rise when others won't. This gives you time to create in the early hours of the morning, time to invest in yourself through learning and doing the work. The flow state that you can get into daily in the peaceful moments of the morning is what accelerates and promotes you to the places you have dreamed about.

Reading daily gives you new ideas. It broadens your thinking and teaches you how to think. Imagine being able to have conversations with anyone in the world. This is the power of books. You can learn through their wisdom and advance your open steps. The effect of reading is profound. All roads lead to acceleration, purpose and growth. You are unlocking future wins every time you read. If you don't like a book, put it down and try another one – use discernment.

Being in tune with all you have to be grateful for is an abundant way to live. Prosperity is attracted to this level of vibration and thought. Don't discount its value and place in your life. As the founder of a business, the captain of the ship, it's on you to be filled to the brim with optimism, creation and enthusiasm for what can happen and then, like a magician, bring it into form through hard work, persistence and doing the basics day in and day out for long enough to have a breakthrough. Your day is coming, so don't quit now.

DIRECTION

REVIEW your goals frequently, 3–5 times a day. This speaks to direction; the more often you see your goals the less you go off track. This is about course correcting, visualising the place you are headed towards, living as if it has already happened, because in your mind it already has. When you familiarise yourself with the feeling of it having happened already, a strange thing happens: it begins to occur in the external world. We have power in our subconscious mind that can interact with divine intelligence and create the future as we see it already.

DESTINATION

IT'S about who you become in the process. The journey is the gift. It's about the opportunities to give back, showing others how it can be through your example. The wins are there, but the true wins are internal. They're the times you wanted to give up but didn't - the times you thought you didn't have it in you, but you showed up anyway and delivered. This is character, this is where you make it. Of course, I'd be lying if I said that the external wins weren't awesome, they are, they are better than you think, because you know what it took to make it happen. You know the early mornings, the grit, and the determination that you put in. But it's the lifestyle you create that is the real gold for you, your family and generations to come.

> "The only real test of intelligence is if you get what you want out of life."
>
> **– NAVAL RAVIKANT**

That's an interesting thought, given Jim Rohn's advice on direction. If getting what we want is the spice of life, then making sure we have a clear goal and act towards that goal should be our primary objective.

Landing the first domino should be yours. You should be able to intuitively sense where you are versus where you need to be to obtain your goal.

Think of it like this: you are a system, and your system is only as good as your ability to iterate and course correct. You fail your way to success. Just like a thermostat adjusts when the door opens and cold air enters a room, you adjust and move forwards based on where you are compared to your goal.

If we take Naval's quote and dissect it, it suggests that low intelligence would be not learning from mistakes, being inflexible and sticking to one process or way of thinking, only to produce suboptimal results. Hard work is not the answer. Instead, you should work hard at course correcting to stay on mission, working towards your goal, reviewing your goals and keeping them front of mind multiple times a day. This is how you condition yourself for success. Having a goal determines how you see the world. Goals are important; therefore, I would encourage you to make landing the first domino your goal. Over the next 90 days I want you to secure this feat.

In the 1950's Dr Maxwell Maltz, the legendary American surgeon and author of the bestselling book *Psycho-Cybernetics* became fascinated by the number of patients who came to him with vastly exaggerated "mental pictures" of their physical deformities. These patients got the surgery to remove the deformity yet some of them remained unhappy, insecure and unchanged despite having the new face they desired. This was intriguing to Maltz. Why did some patients have radical improvements to their wellbeing, happiness and self-esteem whilst others showed no improvement? His findings showed that it had to do with the mental picture they carried of themselves, their programming.

Cybernetics is the art of getting what you want. It comes from the Greek word *'kybernētēs',* which means "to steer" or "good at steering". When Maltz worked with athletes, salespeople, you name it, it was the mental programming that dictated whether they were conditioned for success.

His work goes on to call out another book *Better Golf Without Practice,* which states that upwards of 90% of the game is mental, 8% is physical and 2% is equipment.

We are goal-seeking beings, and the mind and body work hand in hand as a system to lock on to your goal. Therefore, we must prime our subconscious minds by visualising the goal already achieved. This is how you train your mindset. Think of your mindset like an internal blueprint that tells you what is possible for you. Therefore, in order to expand our results, we must first expand what we believe is possible, realistic and likely to happen for us.

The way to improve this blueprint is to improve our self-image. This is the thermostat in our lives. We never get hotter or colder than what we believe we can achieve based on our self-image. Therefore, we must continually seek to upgrade our self-image by focusing our attention on where we are headed, our sense of purpose and mission, having courage, giving to others, living meaningful values, acting as the person we want to become and increasing our self-confidence by doing what we say we will. Keeping our promises to ourselves is a massive way to boost your confidence and self-esteem.

Likewise, diminishing limiting beliefs, negative self-talk and pessimism should be mandatory action from now on. You will walk in the light and have high standards for yourself. No longer will you tolerate mediocrity. You are on a mission and you are fine-tuned for success. This new operating system will guide you towards your goal of landing your first domino and many more to come, but it starts by taking the first step, creatively overcoming challenges and heading in the direction you want to go. This is the success-achieving mechanism.

THE BASIC FUNDAMENTALS

NEVER take your eye off the obvious metrics for predicting success. You want a full pipeline, you want to simplify and not make things overly complex. If there's something you can do to potentially bring in business now, you should do it. Procrastination is what kills most ideas. Instead, you need to flip it and follow that badass idea, ping that person, reach out, buy all the muffins and push forward. What's the worst that could happen? They don't respond? The worst thing would be not sending anything and missing out on the first domino that could have changed your whole business and life trajectory.

Build your "do it now" muscle. What would an outperforming salesperson's pipeline look like? It would be healthy, overflowing, abundant, ripe. There are so many clues as to the identity of the person playing out in business. If you are not killing it right now, you've got to go out and create that reality. It starts from within and how you see the world.

Keep your pipeline healthy, know your conversion rate, and work the maths. The data is there, so use it.

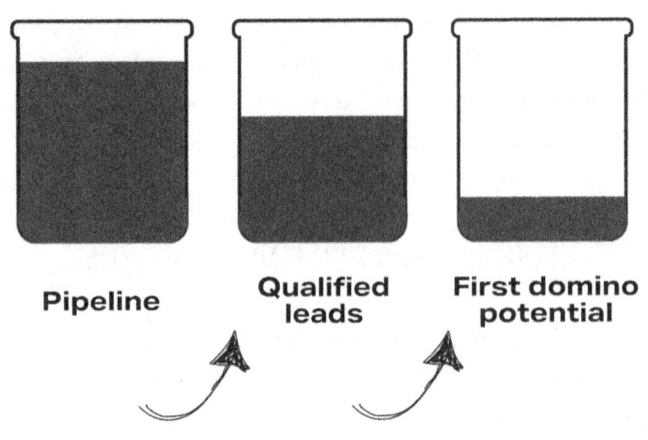

THE FIRST DOMINO

Pipeline → Conversion rate 1 → **Qualified leads** → Conversion rate 2 → **First domino potential**

Then get after it. You don't have to keep doing your business the way you always have; you set the tempo, you set the risk appetite, you are the barometer and the wind in your sails. You have far more going for you than you give yourself credit for. These clients want you and what you have, but you were just not asking the right questions, putting yourself in the right places or making the right moves to be in the rhythm. Now you are armed with a different approach, a way to cut through the noise and break the mould. Step into this new phase of your business with all the might and strength of a hero coming home from battle.

"Talent hits a target no one else can hit;
genius hits a target no one else can see."

– AUTHUR SCHOPENHAUER

CHAPTER 10: BECOME A MAGNET

TODAY'S DOMINO CHALLENGE

Go back and re-read the last few pages on Cause, Effect, Direction and Destination. It takes five minutes but will change your life if implemented consistently.

This is the operating system that will help to shape your destiny. Be rigorous in your commitment to self-improvement. Be all in.

Take the next 90 days and continue to channel winning energy. Vibrate higher, as if you've already landed a handful of your dream clients. Take each day, every decision, every conversation in the spirit of this certainty: the goal has already been achieved.

As a reminder these are your operating principles for the next 90 days.

- Go to bed at 9–9.30pm every night, get up at 4.30–5am every morning.
- Exercise daily and make it a part of your identity.
- Read 10–20 pages per day.
- Write down new ideas as they appear.
- Note down all you have to be grateful for in your phone.
- Review your goals 3–5 times a day.
- Live as if your goal has already happened in attitude and mind.
- Remember, it's about who you become in the process.
- The lifestyle you create is the real gold.

CHAPTER 11
CREATE YOUR ECONOMY

WHEN the first domino falls more will follow, thick and fast. But know this, it will be because of who've you become, your character, the respect you have for yourself, and your ability to not be controlled by the outcome.

In sales, as in life, you are always creating your own economy. Once you decide what you want and live it, as that person, surrounding yourself with mentors that shape your thinking and actions, it all comes together. Your attitude, character and standard are what shapes the trajectory of your economy, but it is never the circumstance. You may have heard the notion that if you took all the money in the world and distributed it equally among every person it wouldn't take long before it was back in the same hands it is currently, those that understand enterprise, the value of network and personal brand. These elements are of vital importance, especially personal brand. It's how George Clooney made more in one day from tequila than his entire acting career; it's how Rihanna earned 95% of her fortune, with only 5% coming from music. Your personal brand is the new currency. It works for you 24/7, developing your network in your sleep and building trust at scale.

The funny thing is that you attract the first domino as if by magic. It's because your awareness has grown so you can spot new opportunities, take new risks, and complete the right actions to bring this domino and many more into your orbit. It will feel effortless in the end because you'll be so focused on what you can give, the value you can bring to the market and creating magic, that the market rewards you with trust. It's the person you become by choosing to be persistent with what you want. To believe and have faith in a vision that you can see and consciously create an environment that's in harmony with the outcome you want. There's a vibrational frequency to success: abundance is non clingy, it doesn't give to get, it's at one with where it is going and values itself.

I hope you see, through the exercises in this book, that when you become better, you attract better. It happens effortlessly, as if by magic, through your commitment to improve daily, to work on yourself and expand your mind. This is the beginning, middle and the end. It's everything.

Only by going through this experience can you release yourself from old patterns, limiting beliefs and any reliance you have on your old self. That is how you create space for the new.

When you take the right actions with the right energy you unlock doors that are right in front of you but have been hidden from view, until you became the person you are now.

Gratitude is a portal through which you attract abundance into your life. Step through it daily and find ways to give to others. Become a giver. When you combine this character with a persistent mental attitude, you tap into a winning spirit that empowers you to new levels of thinking.

You create the circumstances for your success, so stop doubting what's possible for you; that burning desire is in you for a reason. There are examples all around you of people who have made it happen and there's no reason that can't be you. Focus on improving yourself, your mindset, your way of viewing circumstances. This is the asymmetric risk. What have you really got to lose? The downside is so much smaller than the potential upside you have when this business takes off.

CHAPTER 11: CREATE YOUR ECONOMY

I know some of you might be on the brink of quitting or thinking that it's not going to happen. You might be thinking what do I have to offer that big client? I'm just a team of one, or three or five people, how can we play in the big leagues? This is where you're wrong. You have everything to offer, because you are nimble, you can pivot quickly and make product customisations that aren't possible as a large behemoth. After all, you aren't weighed down by internal politics and layers of red tape. You are hungrier, and you want it more. You have the biggest advantage. You are everything they need: the innovation, the bleeding edge, the ability to integrate fresh ideas and the opportunity to make a difference in the world. You deserve to walk into that boardroom and make your case, to consult and add a ton of value. Never let the circumstances and fear of being new to the job or new to the industry take over. Don't let the thoughts about the size of your company or state of your product development or lack of clients keep you from adding value.

If you're the founder of a company, this is where you must push harder, to stop these doubts in their tracks, to know that you deserve to be in every room. You need to work on your self-esteem and character, your belief in yourself, so that you can seize the opportunity in front of you. You'll be surprised at what you can achieve when you believe you are supposed to be there, when you recognise the actual reality is that they need you. When you see it, you can't unsee it. They need you.

You have value to offer; you are a merchant of value creation, of conversations that inspire action and change within an organisation. Plant good seeds, and they will multiply. Everything you do has an effect. Results or lack thereof can't get you down, so keep persisting. Give value. Put it out into the world. Share enthusiasm in someone's business, keep helping others in your network by making useful referrals and introducing them to others. Help someone get that new role, and in the process be a source of value in all areas; become someone who's good to know.

This is where the tide changes and you get into a new level of network and value. It's where you multiply your results. There's an energy to success and sales - rainmakers know this. When that first domino tips and you land that first client, celebrate hard, then get back to work. Don't let the joy of success let you take your foot off the gas or deviate from the high leverage sales process that you have installed.

You create your economy. The opportunity for a quantum leap is right in front of you. For those that want to learn more about quantum leaps I wholeheartedly recommend you read you^2 by Price Pritchett. As defined below by Oxford Languages, a quantum leap is a sudden increase in something, a rapid advance. For example, the number of clients you are landing...

noun
1. a huge, often sudden, increase or advance in something.

This is what happens once the first domino falls. You make a dramatic advance into a new level, achieving breakthroughs in your personal effectiveness too.

As we conclude this journey together, I want to make one last ditch attempt to ensure you fully realise your role as a salesperson with your clients.

Whether you are the CEO and founder of your business or a sales leader looking for transformation, there's one thing that I hope has been made clear throughout this book. It's that you are there to add value to your clients and you do this by how you interact with them.

Imagine your best friend came to you and they were in the

market for whatever it is your company sells. How would you treat them differently to how you are currently treating your clients?

Would you be more honest, open and candid about what's on offer? Would you try to push them towards the high cost package or would you help them through the process by giving them just what they needed, allowing them to expand once they understood how your solutions worked? Would you have their back and their best interests at heart?

The truth is, if it was your best friend, you'd lay it out authentically, openly and with honesty, because you'd want them to make the best decision for themselves. That decision can only be made when they are aware of the pitfalls, what can go wrong, the realistic timelines and the challenges in advance. You'd be less focused on your commission or winning their business for the profit alone. In behaving this way, your best friend would naturally feel supported, coached through the process by a trusted ally, and more likely take your recommendations as gold.

Examine your client relationship and how you view your role as a salesperson in the interaction. When you have the right intentions, sales is fun and enjoyable. As the trusted advisor, it takes the pressure off, transforming the discussion into an exciting and elevated conversation.

I had Matt Dixon (co-author of *The Jolt Effect* and *The Challenger Sale*) on the show, and he shared some data that blew me away. He and his team conducted analysis of 2.5 million sales calls captured from Gong and Chorus recordings, and what they found was astounding. 40-60% of a salesperson's qualified leads end up in closed / lost category due to there having been no decision on the part of the client! Can you believe it? 40-60% of your pipeline is not converting because of indecision! This means that the energy output on all fronts is massive and that, if we understand why this is happening, we can triage it and significantly increase our closed / won deal flow.

Do you want to know the real reason customers don't move forward?

Stay with me, you are going to want to hear this: here's what they found. Matt set out to answer two questions. Why do customers make no decision? What do the best salespeople do to avoid that?

If you asked any salesperson, most of them would tell you that a customer not making a decision is, in fact, making a decision. They are deciding not to move forward; they are choosing to stay with the status quo. What they found was that most salespeople had been taught to overcome their inertia with their status quo bias. When the client seems hesitant to move forward, 75% of salespeople dial up the FOMO in a bid to get them to proceed.

This is the correct move, as Matt explored in his previous book, *The Challenger Sale*. Overcoming the status quo bias is a necessary step in the sales process.

Here are three ways he shares to do this:

- Paint the picture of the positive future, of the benefits gained from implementing the solution and the outcomes.
- Increase fear uncertainty and doubt (FUD) and dial up the cost to inaction. For example, we are working with your competitors and they are getting the benefits of working with us. I would hate for you to be left behind.
- Offer discounts with a hard deadline, for example, I have approval to offer you a 10% discount, but you must sign before the end of this week.

But what Matt found that was critical was that these strategies backfired when a client had expressed a desire to move forward but *then* they became hesitant, which is totally surprising.

Why did these sales strategies to provoke FOMO actually make it worse and more likely to result in indecision with this particular subset of clients? The answer was twofold.

Get ready for some jaw dropping data. Matt and his team discovered that in 44% of cases the reason for indecision was a preference for the status quo; the clients were content and they didn't see the value in change. But that wasn't the biggest reason, oh no. The biggest reason by far was a fear of failure! This accounted for 56% of all no-decision losses.

There are some deep-routed psychological factors going on here. What it boils down to is the omission bias. The omission bias is trying to avoid blame.

The interesting part comes when we think about loss. There are two ways we can do this.

In the context of sales, an error of omission is when you choose to stay with your current vendor and, as a result, experience a loss. Another example would be if you chose not to implement groundbreaking technology and then lost market share to your competitor. You are choosing not to do anything, to sit on the sidelines and not make the change. For some reason, this bias is easier to take than when we actively pursue a change and then lose.

The opposite of this is an error of commission, whereby you make a decision and then you experience a loss. For example, you decide not to sell your stocks after a gigantic rally and then the next day they suffer a large drop.

Now, we are at the root cause of why 40-60% of your pipeline is dead in the water. It has to do with the power of not wanting to be blamed when things go wrong. This is what is responsible for the indecision demonstrated by your clients.

People would rather be responsible for a loss from doing

nothing, than from one where they made a decision. This bias is playing out with your clients. They don't want to be held responsible for making a decision if things don't go as planned, even if that is part of their role and responsibility.

Crikey! This is huge! Think back to a time when your gut instinct was telling you to move forward but you held back for fear of making a mistake. This happens in investments, business opportunities, business decisions, and in all manner of areas, including sales.

Now we know this, we need to liberate our clients by guiding them through the process of diminishing their fear around what could go wrong. In essence, they need to know we have their back throughout and not just up until the paperwork is signed.

If you have clients that are sitting on the sidelines, this is more than likely occurring. The fear of messing up is present.

Matt explains you've got to pass through two stage gates with a customer in the sales process. Firstly, you've got to answer the "why change?" question and dial up the FOMO so that they understand the pain of staying the same is worse than doing nothing at all.

But secondly, once you've overcome their bias to do nothing, the customer is now going to start worrying about what could go wrong. This is where you need to dive in and, as the salesperson, your role is to figure out what they are specifically concerned about. Let's be clear, fear of failure means being culpable for the poor performance of your product or service after they made a business case for it and got it implemented. It means that it didn't do what it was supposed to, or that it failed to meet expectations internally. This all blows back on your customer. It damages their reputation and personal brand, career progression and their hip pocket. This is the real reason they prefer not to do anything. What's interesting with this is that the team found three common sources for a customer's fear of failure.

CHAPTER 11: CREATE YOUR ECONOMY

- Firstly, it could be that there are too many options to choose from. Maybe you have a range of solutions and packages, and they are basically fatigued from the possible combinations and ways to work together. It is your responsibility to guide them through this and take some options off the table. Leaving them to decide will end in no decision because they are already overwhelmed.

- Alternatively, it could be their need to constantly feel like the expert and be ahead of the game so that they aren't surprised or blindsided by a change further down the line. "Can you send me just one more whitepaper, one more case study? But what if this happens? How about that?" On and on. They are always needing to worry about the next thing and whether they missed something. This is where you must step in, or else it will spiral and there will never be enough information in this ever-changing world to help them make the decision on their own. Take control of the dialogue and expertly guide them towards the right path to choose. They need to know you are in the game, and there for them.

- Finally, they found that expectations overload is holding customers back. This is where customers are questioning if they will see the full ROI for the product or service. They are totally bought in, but they just doubt that, for their specific use case, it's going to deliver the results as expected. This is a big one. Put yourself in the buyer's shoes; they go get approval, fight for your company to be in the mix and then it doesn't deliver. Who's in the firing line then? Them, that's who!

Now we are getting to the heart of the matter regarding why deals just vanish into thin air, even as they were about to sign the contract. I bet some of you who are reading this are just nodding. You get it. Those deals where they were super keen, they get your value, they enjoy working with you and you've got everything ready to go. It's just the final signature that you're waiting on, but then it seems to slow down, messages become less frequent, and it feels like all of the air has gone out of the balloon. Well, now you know why. It's because it has! It left out of the back door with its friends, fear and anxiety, while you were sharpening your pen and getting the contract ready. Don't be fooled into thinking this isn't happening in your deals.

So, now we know what the client is secretly thinking, how do we change this?

CHAPTER 12
SECURING YOUR FIRST DOMINO

When it comes to influencing the prospect to make a decision, to move forward, to sign the deal, what do you think the biggest factor is?

I'll give you a hint; it's not about you.

Most salespeople think that it's about how confidently they present the pitch, and they'd be right. There's a huge element of being confident and having conviction that influences another party.

You need to have conviction and belief in what you are doing, of course. This is in order to transfer that belief to the prospect, but the needle-mover here is how confident the prospect feels about their decision. When the prospect feels solid, in and of themselves, they have made their mind up. They have convinced themselves. Therefore, in conjunction with confidence, we must also solve for this.

It's true, your results are linked to your confidence, which is linked to your self-image. If you want different results, then you must increase your self-image.

But what about the prospect?

Have you ever faced a big decision and been unsure? I have. Have you ever gone forward with that same decision and then felt heaps of regret afterward?

Yup, I've been there, done that, got the t-shirt (and full suit).

It's not pleasant, it feels energy-draining every time you think of that purchase, bad move, or alternative option. Guess what?

THE FIRST DOMINO

It's happened to everyone you are trying to sell to as well. Every prospect you want to bring into your business, to be your first domino, has had this experience. Whether in a complex business decision, job offer, or a large purchase, they will have progressed forward with a deal, not being fully convinced within themselves, and then later wrestled with the sting of regret.

They know what that feels like, to make an error, to be held accountable by the management team, in some cases their job and reputation would've been on the line. When the prospect isn't fully convinced in themselves, doubt creeps in, they make mistakes, and the implementation steps don't have the backing required to make it a successful engagement.

Therefore, if you are with a prospect and doing a deal and you sense that they aren't 100% into it, if they are conflicted, unsure and feel hesitation but you convince them to go forward, what do you think happens?

Well, for starters, a few days later they call with buyer's remorse and try to backtrack or renegotiate the terms. They are looking to bail. That is not ideal; it's a time waster for everyone.

We know that every experienced client has been through this in their life, even if they are not yet in business. They've been through it for sure in their personal lives.

Just like you and me, they have scars from it. It stings, it causes apprehension, PTSD. They want to avoid making the same mistake in the future. This uncertainty is playing out in your sales and dealmaking process today.

It doesn't have to be this way. It can be eradicated by shining a light on the uncertainty, asking the questions that others fear to ask. Or going into the cave that holds the treasure we seek (thanks, Joseph Campbell!).

How do we mitigate this in every deal then?

The way to do this is by influencing how confident the prospect

CHAPTER 12: SECURING YOUR FIRST DOMINO

feels about doing a deal with you. We must get under the hood, to what's really holding them back, and confidently aid them to navigate this uncertainty, without digging into what's going on for them. We lose deals because the pain of making a mistake is too great, or we force them to move forward, and they hop off the train at the next station. To avoid this, we must peel back the layers of the onion and go where salespeople rarely tread. Truly confident operators don't fear finding out hard truths, dispelling myths, having uncomfortable conversations and working on behalf of their clients to help them to recognise the next best step to take.

Do they get that you understand them? Do they truly feel it? Are you willing to go into the cave with them and ask the tough questions, to shine a light on the thing they fear and address it? You need to; the alternative is that they don't buy. But the upside is monumentally big.

The prospect will sign if they feel confident in themselves. This is what we want to solve for them. We want to help a prospect to recognise in themselves that they are confident about doing this deal as the right way forward. The decision to act comes from them.

Your prospect wants to look great internally, not like an incompetent fool, so you need to reassure them that doing this deal will make them look like a hero to their company. And you need to have a plan to support this too. They need to feel that you'll have their back and go all the way. You need to give them reassurance and guarantees to show them how it is going to work through the stages of implementation. Give them a road map on how you will work together, and flesh it out, step by step, with dates. This is what counts. This is what brings down their anxiety and demonstrates that you are their trusted advisor. This is the space where you want to play. Your role is to help them feel confident in their decision, to make them feel awesome about it.

This is where you build trust, and that's how you can build an impenetrable reputation for yourself. When the market trusts you, which is something no one can take from you, the respect you have for yourself to do good business that's good for the prospect only grows.

To better understand this, let's look at a few things salespeople do that makes it harder for a prospect to feel confident in themselves. Memorise this list and make sure that this isn't you!

- Information overload – in seeing that the prospect is unsure, they throw more information at them, in the hope that it will help them to feel safer and convince them. Instead, this leads to information overload. Hello, overwhelm central and decision fatigue! Instead, get to the root cause of the issue, it's inside your prospect, and triage that.

- Packages, products and services overload – prospects hesitate because there are too many options, there's too many ways to cut the cake. Prospects need a very simple implementation roadmap that has been validated against their specific concerns. Trying to force them to eat everything all at once leads to stagnation and avoidance.

- Making the deal too complex – my goodness, this is a massive problem because deal complexity reduces confidence. Clarity leads to confidence. Keep it simple, folks.

- Not addressing the uncertainty that the prospect is likely feeling. As a salesperson, it is your job to close this gap. You need to help them to overcome uncertainty by demonstrating that you are the trusted advisor, sharing stories and experiences of what you've seen happen before and lighting their path.

CHAPTER 12: SECURING YOUR FIRST DOMINO

⚅ There are often conflicting messages and ambiguity that is left there untouched, like a side dish on the table that nobody wants, but everyone can see it. Marketing and Sales can be at odds with messaging. Make sure your message is on point and aligns with a specific intention and goal of your doing business together.

The reason I bring this up at this exact stage is because you are close to landing that first domino and making the difference that you've been wanting for so long.

The thing I want to impress upon you is that you have what it takes to land this client and more and you can do it in a way that magnifies your character, multiplies and accelerates your future results and leaves you free to fully celebrate the win. Go into the cave if you sense their uncertainty. Your clients will respect you for it.

Your conviction will rub off on your prospect, but it can't be your only strategy. You must have this and more. It's the unattachment to the outcome that leaves room for the feeling of abundance to enter the room.

YOUR GIFTS, TALENTS AND SKILL

THINK about this, you have unique skills and talents that were given to you. They are yours to help you produce, to do business and to be prosperous.

The more you can focus on getting better every day, improving how you interact with your prospects, the better. It can't feel like you are hunting them down on the Serengeti, only that you are interested in them as people.

When given the opportunity, would you mess this up? Say you

run into your ideal stakeholder at a conference, would you know what to say, or would you wing it?

> "For things to get better, you've got to get better. Don't wish it were easier, wish you were better. Just ask that you can get wiser and stronger and better and be able to take care of your own responsibilities. Get better."
>
> **– JIM ROHN**

It's your creativity that is the key. It's you shining as you, knowing your stuff but also having the courage and confidence to shine a light on all areas of the deal, even the parts that don't look so rosy, to own it, the good, the bad and the not ready yet. Sales is the transfer of belief, and belief comes from within. You can feel it and so can they. When you can go there, it produces trust. Rather than brushing over sticking points, clean them up and shine.

This is where the spirit of collaboration comes in. What happens when they ask a tricky question because of the circumstances? The circumstances are that you are a startup, or you don't have a proven or credible client base, testimonials, or any other number of things they think they need to move forward. It's a test, so don't fail by getting frustrated or flustered. This is easy to do when you are expecting the question, so expect the question.

When they ask, "Do you have any clients yet? Who are you working with?"

You answer, "We're on the journey with Zeecars, Openbook and Doyourthing.com."

The key here is not to give in (mentally) to the objection that

CHAPTER 12: SECURING YOUR FIRST DOMINO

the client is getting at here, which is whether they can trust you, whether you have credibility in this space. You have to tell them who else thinks what you are selling is a phenomenal idea. You must answer this question honestly, openly and enthusiastically.

Or, if they start the conversation skeptically (as most do when you are a startup innovating and breaking new ground), "Well, what you are doing? It's not really a thing here, is it? It's a very new market. Is anyone working with you?"

The first thing you do is agree. By agreeing, you get them to lean in, so you say, "I know what you mean. You are right. I thought that it was a new space, but now, after seeing who is leaning in, I'll tell you that it's the big clients. They are all aware they need to make a change in X and they're already taking steps to do Y."

This way of responding does so in a way that makes them not feel offended. You are agreeing that they are right to assume that but then carefully go on to reveal some new information that suggests they are misinformed. However, by agreeing, it allows you both to save face. You are saying, "I also was like you. I also thought that... until." This way lays the foundations for you to build your case and move the prospect forward, to reveal new data points. It sets the conversation in motion in a way that's constructive, together, collaborative, honest and understanding.

Yes, we are a new company, in an entirely new space, and guess what? That's great because we are moving with the times, disrupting a legacy system and building the future. This turns what could be a conversation stopper (if handled defensively), into an exciting projection for the future, of working together to build something special that adds unique value to their business.

The reason I am bringing these questions up now is because, right when you get to the end of the sales process and you are about to sign the client, often a new stakeholder will be brought into the discussion. This might not be planned, you might have done all your stakeholder mapping, thought that you met and influenced everyone only to find out that, right at the end, there's one more decision maker to get over the line.

A question like this, if answered flustered, causes tension, resistance and blocks your path.

Questions that are difficult to answer at any point in the sales process will get asked and you must be able to get to the heart of them. What's the thing that they are needing, the feeling they are looking to either resolve (doubt, reluctance) or amplify (trust, safety, connection)?

"I need proof points and case studies of how we have done this in other markets, please share them with me."

"As you're a startup, can you do it for free? Do you offer a free test? I need something to get stakeholders to buy in."

Your answers and energy when answering these questions is going to either create more uncertainty in the client's mind or leave them feeling at ease and leaning in. Obviously, we want the latter, but we want this to be the outcome *every time* and that's where practising this skill comes in. There's a finesse to it. When you are answering these questions, you welcome them. It's not probing deeper for the sake of it, and if done incorrectly, with bluntness, objectiveness or a reaction that stinks of defensiveness, you will put the deal back significantly. Even if they get a sniff of your desire to resolve their uncertainty, so you can get what you want, not what they want, they will close up and the conversation will cease.

This is all playing out in your conversations. It's just that we don't bring awareness to it. We think the deal didn't progress because they didn't have the budget, the timing wasn't right, or there wasn't a product fit, but often the real reason remains hidden because the salesperson fails to use this skill correctly and, in attempting to dig into their hesitation because they read it in a book or heard on a podcast that it was a good idea, they inadvertently blow up the deal with their unprepared approach and undeveloped skill.

Instead, we must respond to any of these questions with a mindset of curiosity, our tone of voice must match this intention. The prospect is looking for cracks, inconsistencies between what we say and how we act. This means your body language, posture and facial expressions must reflect genuine curiosity, as if their question caused you no offence, didn't make you panic, or flinch, because it didn't.

Instead, you can use these questions as an opportunity to insert humor into your conversation, to get real with the prospect, to level with them, to tell them how it is and to ask questions back to them. It's an opportunity for you to probe deeper with them. To gather information.

"Can I ask you, what would you look for in a company that's doing X?"

"What might be included as part of your decision criteria?"

"How would this affect your outcomes?"

"If you could have anything, what are your desired capabilities for a product like this?"

"I love that you brought that up, how would you approach it?"

When you use these questions as a springboard into new territory, you outpace the competition.

SELF-WORTH

YOUR self-esteem also comes into it. It's where you make the very journey you are on, with the exact advantage being that it opens up new doors and lands you more clients than you can handle.

Prepare yourself to be asked these tricky questions and answer them with grace, openness and authenticity. This is why you need to know what it is you are aiming for. What is the number one thing you want for your business (or KPIs) right now?

Are you prioritising network effects and adoption, revenue, or profit, case studies or new logos, what is most important? If you are a new salesperson joining a new team, you'll most likely want to demonstrate that they made a great decision by showing revenue impact as quickly as possible. Whereas, if you are in a new business role, it might be going after new logos for the customer success team to nurture and develop over the course of the year. Whatever success means to you, it should feed into what you want.

When you don't get offended by questions, and instead answer confidently, it shows respect for your business and purpose. Don't shy away, instead move the conversation towards things that boost the confidence of the prospect and speak to some of their psychological drivers for change and action.

These are high leverage things like:

- First mover advantage – to gain market share and take new ground.
- Thought leadership – those in senior positions understand the value of taking a stance on a particular topic. They have a responsibility to lead the way, to walk the talk, shine a light on those who want to be seen.
- PR that can be generated from working together – most clients love the world to know they are doing game-changing work, both as the company and on the personal level. Don't miss this opportunity to tap into some of these big psychological motivators. People want to increase their status.
- Purpose – all organisations have an impact and purpose

CHAPTER 12: SECURING YOUR FIRST DOMINO

that can be tapped into. Leverage these commitments and values to influence action.

- Innovation – most organisations know this is the life blood of new revenue streams and will have a portion of the budget set aside for this very reason.
- Promotion – think about your prospect's short-term and long-term goals. How can what you do help your prospect get promoted or increase their status? What can you do to make them look like a hero in their company and also make their lives easier?

If the conversation ever stalls or gets awkward when they talk about price, a simple reframe back to value is where you need to focus their attention. This is not about what it costs, it's about the outcome they want to achieve. If this outcome happens, would you be willing to do X? This is especially important if top-line revenue is your goal; any conversation about price should be brought back to value. Once you go down the road of offering free trials, they automatically discount the value you are providing. It's a psychological no-no.

Don't go there thinking that you can turn the tables later once they understand how great your product and services are. Maintain your pricing strategy, hold your ground, feel confident in the fact that you offer value. That's why you are here.

Self-esteem and self-worth plays out in these conversations all the time. I recommend you watch the TED Talk, *What I learned from 100 days of rejection* by Jia Jiang. It's an enjoyable fifteen-minute talk that I believe will inspire you to break out of your routine, as per Chapter 2, and do things that other people think are impossible.

Here's a photo of me lying down in the middle of Starbucks, training my 7-year-old son how to not give a crap what anyone

THE FIRST DOMINO

thinks (he's taking the pic). The purpose was to demonstrate rejection therapy in real life.

Courtesy of Levi Lopez Castle

It's about generating momentum in the market and then leveraging this momentum to bring in new clients.

Talk about clients leaning in, and conversations being in the works. Own it all and celebrate it.

As the founder, your responsibility is to be proud of the work you are doing and the clients that are leading the way. Don't let the questions from the client throw you off. If handled correctly, you will show them that working together creates a vast opportunity. Speak possibility and life into your deals.

When you sweep their tough questions under the carpet and don't address them, it doesn't help the client feel more confident. If anything, they come to their own conclusion that they were right. This is not an assumption you want.

CHAPTER 12: SECURING YOUR FIRST DOMINO

Similarly – by not taking the time to unpack and explore their difficult questions, you miss out on the opportunity to learn, connect and refocus.

This is the BIG one. When a client is too gung-ho, too enthusiastic right from the start and they make it sound like you are going to do the deal of the century with no issues, no need for tough questions, it's all good. However, as soon as they get back to the office, it's crickets, and you don't hear a peep from them.

I've seen this countless times. What's going on here? I think you know the answer: you didn't go into the cave. Re-read the above and implement. There's no need to explain this further, just be aware that if it sounds too good it probably is, and if a client is asking tough questions, they may be much closer to buying than you think. This likelihood increases, especially when you welcome their questions and, in turn, make them feel more at ease, allowing them to develop conviction within themselves.

As a salesperson, your character, integrity and intentions are all on display all of the time, whether you think they are or not. Therefore, it's imperative that you live as a person you respect, do what you say you are going to do and share it. By sharing it, it allows the prospect to develop deeper bonds and likeability.

If you get this right, you'll be able to understand what your champion wants, what motivates them. For instance, are they looking to understand a new area? If so, you can help them upskill in your field.

When we focus on them, we start to fine tune our detection ability. Done with enough frequency, you'll start to spot trends and quickly refine your skills to identify what motivates them. Do they want a raise, or a promotion, to boost their reputation? Are they looking for connections, to make more money, to make an impact, to fulfil a cause, to support a purpose? What are their core beliefs? Do they believe in innovation?

Your aim should be to get to the core of who they are and what they believe in – ask yourself what drives them.

- What KPIs do they have?
- What are they wanting to achieve in the next two years?
- What are they pushing for in the short term (next six months)?
- What projects are they passionate about (in and outside of work)?
- What activities do they do in their spare time?

You'll uncover such interesting stories that you couldn't have predicted beforehand. They might share they are building an international property portfolio on the side and are thinking to leave in 12 months' time. This is how you become a super connector. Now you know someone with this skillset and, the next time you meet a person looking to venture into the same area, you have a place to send them. It's all valuable data. When you do this enough, you'll spot the trends and you'll see ways to help others and add value. It will be effortless. This is all about awareness; the more you do this, the more ways you'll realise you can assist.

Oftentimes, entrepreneurs and salespeople aren't having enough high-quality conversations. It's when you go below the surface, get to know the person behind the role and the title, that's where the magic happens. It's when they share their goals, dreams and aspirations with you.

Watch yourself as you have conversations this week. How deep are you getting? What real insight did you glean from each interaction? Ask yourself, am I just going through the motions? It's a good idea to keep track of the questions your prospects ask. This will help you craft better answers for the future as well as provide you with new marketing content. These topics are ones

CHAPTER 12: SECURING YOUR FIRST DOMINO

that prospects need help clarifying. They point towards their fears, worries and doubts. By orientating your marketing, content and FAQs, it helps to bring down the walls and define you as the expert. By bringing awareness to how deep you are getting, it will help you to avoid mediocre patterns of questioning behaviour and conversations that only go surface level. This will level up the quality of your prospecting process. The awareness is the key. Once you become aware of your current questioning style, you can make changes to course correct. It changes it from automatic to conscious awareness and that's where you can interrupt the pattern and create new strategies to go deeper.

Plant good seeds and you'll reap a fruitful harvest. Go into every meeting with your standards high, your intention locked on a mindset of service and deep discovery, and you'll enrich those around you and, in return, live richly.

Proverbs 11:25 says, "A generous person will prosper, whoever refreshes others will be refreshed."

You may be the underdog as a startup, but what's cooler than an underdog that's connecting others, giving as they go. They are a change agent tuned into creating momentum for those around them and also kicking ass in the meantime. This is what leads to a really big life.

It's when we stop trying to care and actually care, unattached to whether we receive something back in return, that we leap to new levels.

When you are meeting with clients, they will bring up topics and needs outside of your business capabilities, and this is the perfect opportunity for you to introduce them to your network. This will inspire your creativity; it will push you out of your comfort zone and bring more into your life.

I want you to win. I am sharing this because, once you start acting in this way and moving with intention, using your creativity,

THE FIRST DOMINO

you'll start to get ideas flowing in all directions. This is yours to follow – it's speaking to you. This is when you should go hard with your prospecting, having conversations, and turn your magic on. The magic comes from inside. When you tap into it, it gives you an edge.

Sales is both an art and a science. It's about being consistent with follow-up, but also creative with your lead generation strategies. One gathering you host could set the biggest deal of your life in motion. You are one act away from the whole of your life changing. Host meet-ups, even if only five people show up and one of them is your mum, it's fine. Who cares?

You are out there making it happen. It's the start, and where it ends up, only you and your desire to make it happen decide. This is your life, your moment to get out there and into the rhythm of success. Everything you want will be attracted to you when you get into the spirit and vibration of it already happening. You must have discipline around your focus. Once you know what you want, you lock in, and you have to be resolute in your commitment; you don't give a flying fuck about distractions.

Everything you do comes from where you are headed; you are living as if the goal has already been achieved. You aren't in comparison or lack, you are dancing to your own beat, throwing the balls up in the air, and now you are juggling. You're loving it. You've got momentum and no one can tell you nothin'.

WHAT IT TAKES

MOST people won't tell you what they do to perform at the highest levels. If you see someone rock up and give an incredible speech, 9 times out of 10 that person will have practised 20-30 times with a dry run. There are, of course, those who can do it on the fly, and

CHAPTER 12: SECURING YOUR FIRST DOMINO

they are really something else. What I don't want you to miss here is that it is OK and perfectly fine to stumble your way to success. Just because it looks like everyone is out there killing it, you need to remember that they are not; they were up to 3am practising, stressing about it, just like you. When you know this, it gives you some solace. Everyone is just making it up, failing upwards; therefore, you can do the same, in *your* own way. Your creativity and your gifts are your secret sauce. Combine them in ways only you can and unlock your next level. Trust your instinct and take action on those opportunities that come to you in a flash of divine guidance.

If you are working in a company, the way to elevate is to have bi-weekly catch ups with the top salespeople in other markets. What this will show you is how they think, as you get to know them better, they'll open up and share details with you. You'll find out what they did to make a pitch, presentation or event look effortless.

Everyone is winging it but also doing the work to elevate their game and develop their abilities. I want you to see how these rainmakers operate so you can cut yourself some slack and enjoy the ride. Failure is growth and growth is winning.

This way you can leverage their learnings and save yourself time. When you put their strategies into motion, you'll avoid the pitfalls because of advice from someone who's already ahead of you.

Similarly, if you are a founder then talking with other founders in the community is incredibly helpful. It's those connections, introductions, and ideas that can only come from getting out there and being part of the scene. Follow that instinct my friend. It is guiding you for a reason.

Everything you want exists and it's yours to receive... doesn't that excite you?

Now, if you're sitting here reading this but secretly thinking, "This is all very well and good, Tim, but what the heck do I do? I am doing all of this already. I know what you are saying but really, it's the prospect's confidence in the deal, my creativity and conviction and my ability to get off my ass and serve others, meet people, say 'yes' to more random events. Yes, yes and heck yes, it's all of this and much more."

These are the steps.

- Recognise where you are.
- Recognise what you truly want.
- Recognise where you aren't doing what could move the needle – events, panels, networking, making introductions, getting into the spirt of the life you want, as if everything has already happened, doing things that are new and kind of scary to you, although they could also be good for business.
- Get off your ass and take action!
- Recognise that you have the opportunity to be a change agent for your industry, for your peers, for the competition, making them sit up and take notice.
- Outsource all tasks that you aren't the absolute best at. Buy back your time so you can focus very clearly on a few set things.
- Set up bi-weekly connections with people who are knocking it out of the park. Hang with those already making it rain. Absorb their strategies and ideas. Action them.
- Take action on your intuition.
- The magic of sales is the transfer of belief. The true king doesn't have to tell people that they are king. The same is true for your incredible product or service.

CHAPTER 12: SECURING YOUR FIRST DOMINO

I know I packed a punch in this short section, but I realised that I was being too nice.

Nice won't get you to recognise the genius that's locked up inside of you, allowing you to act upon it. If this is what it takes to help you to breakthrough, stop getting distracted by everything the world tells you is important and just get moving, then so be it.

A final word on this – there are a lot of redundancies taking place all the time and, as the world evolves, this will continue. Many people are out of work. You need to think like an A player by thinking long term. If there are people in your industry that you can help find new jobs, get out there and make the connection.

I'll tell you a short story: Steven was working on a lucrative RFP for a gigantic client. This deal had the potential to make his whole year's target. This would certainly earn him a promotion and a hefty commission. More than that, it would establish him as a rainmaker in the company, a rising talent on the way to the top and one to watch. Part-way through the RFP process, Steven's main point of contact and champion at the client got made redundant. Steven kept working on the RFP and didn't think much about it, only that it was a shame that all the time and work they had invested into this stakeholder was now lost.

Then he got a call from his boss that taught him an important lesson. The call went like this: "Hey Steven, can you give me Paul's phone number? I want to call him."

Steven, a little surprised, replied, "Sure, but you do know he's no longer working on this RFP, don't you? He's been made redundant."

Steven's boss said something that he would never forget. "Yes, that's right. I want to reach out to him and see if I can help in any way. You never know where people will end up. He will come back and be in a great position one day soon."

Steven was flabbergasted and amazed, both at the same time.

Of course, this was it, by being a caring person, offering your help, making an introduction here and a recommendation there, showing through your actions who you are, it makes a difference in the long term.

The lesson impacted Steven and he thought differently about how to offer a helping hand in the lives of others from that day onwards. It's vital to recognise that their ways to give also enable you to differentiate yourself, be there for others and make a difference.

I encourage you to reach out to people in your wider network when you hear that they have been made redundant and help them through their tough times. You never know where people end up. It might be years later that this person comes back into your life, and because you reached out, because you were there in their darkest hour and their time of need, they will remember that. People move into new positions of influence all the time.

Life has a funny way of rewarding those that make good things happen for others. Get out there and make magic happen. You aren't doing this to get rewards. That is just a beautiful side benefit. You are doing this to help someone in a bad time, because it is how you operate. Make it a rule to call people when someone dies, when they lose their job, to lift people up, but never with the intention of getting anything in return. Set your magic on fire and get moving.

No one else will do this consistently, so this will differentiate you. It separates you from the pack. Very few people will reach out to offer help and support. Of course, some friends will. But I am talking about taking it a step further. People move around, they will end up in powerful strategic roles that can be of interest to you in the future. Don't miss this opportunity to be a game changer for others.

CHAPTER 12: SECURING YOUR FIRST DOMINO

TODAY'S DOMINO CHALLENGE

I want you to reach out to someone in your network. Maybe they have been made redundant. I want you to call them up and see how you can help them out.

It could be:

- Making an introduction that inspires a new job offer, partnership, referral, friendship.

- Looking out for relevant roles on their behalf and sending them through, showing that you care by actually caring.

- Being a shoulder for them to lean on, someone to talk to. Oftentimes, just having a key person in your corner makes all the difference.

- Sending them interesting articles, books, podcasts. Anytime something grabs you and you think "this is meant for them". Trust your intuition and send it through.

Send a gift, be a thoughtful individual, lift others up. Make a difference in someone's life today because it is who you are – not because of what you'll get in return.

FINAL WORD

YOU are here with the biggest opportunity in front of you. You are spinning around on this earth standing on a ball of molten rock that burns at over 3,000 degrees Celsius, in the middle of a universe with two trillion galaxies (that's 200 billion [2x10] to the power of eleven) with 200 billion trillion stars in it. Right now, the earth is moving at 67,000 miles per hour. Miraculous things are happening all the time and all you've got to do is land your first domino.

When you zoom out and realise the magnitude of the opportunity that's in front of you, the unlimited potential and upside that can come from actually putting these core principles into practice, then it's all to play for.

I don't mean to minimise the task at hand, far from it, but what I want you to get is that you are a game changer. You are here to do big things and live that big life. This is all yours for the taking.

Just like the Winklevoss twins, yes, those two dudes from the movie *The Social Network,* they had to figure it out when they first heard about Bitcoin at a party in Ibiza in the summer of 2012.

Once back in the US, they set about doing their research and went deep, by March 2013, they were ready to seize the opportunity and sank a cool $11 million of their fortune into Bitcoin. The average closing price in the month of March 2013 was $55.58. Fast forward 12 years, and Bitcoin is now trading at $99,040, up 1781 times and the twins are now worth $5 billion each, at the time of writing.

This is not about whether you like them or not, the point is that they were willing to take a bet they had conviction in. This is the same as the business you've decided to put your all into, whether this be for a company or striking out on your own.

It is all possible.

CHAPTER 12: SECURING YOUR FIRST DOMINO

There are those that go out into the world and do what needs to be done because it is their God given purpose, and there are those that tread water never risking or dreaming big because they let everyone else tell them how to live.

So, we finish where we started with me telling you to have a long hard look in the mirror and asking yourself what you are here to make happen with this short time you have here. It's a gift, a flash in the pan in the scheme of eternity, but it's your moment. Don't let the distractions, doubts of others or the voice inside your head stop you from achieving what's yours.

You must tune in and take ownership over the conversations you have with yourself on a daily basis. You get to choose the thoughts you have and are in complete control over how you perceive the world to be. Set your intentions and think accordingly.

Stay focused on living for your own values, purpose and mission. This is what matters and truly gives fulfilment. When you cultivate and take care of your inner world, making that the centre of your focus by not letting the desires of others intrude, you win at the game of life. As a salesperson and entrepreneur, this matters even more.

Do what brings your heart joy, what inspires you to get up and take action and gives you energy. Sever ties with anything that drains it.

We get lost when we take our focus off our internal world and instead give more power to the external by letting others make our decisions. When likes, follows and validation through prestige, awards and recognition become more important than our inner purpose-driven goals, it's the end of our dreams.

This dampens our appetite for risk and for going all in because we are at the whims of outside approval. We fear not receiving their validation and therefore get stuck. We can't move for fear of rejection or disagreement. We place how others feel about us before how we feel about ourselves, and this act causes us to lose our way. Our compass leans off centre.

I am here to tell you to choose yourself. To boldly pursue the path that you envision, to free yourself from the need to care what anyone else thinks about your business or ambitions. We re-centre by getting close to the source, to tuning in and listening deeply to that voice and yearning inside.

When we don't live authentic to our purpose, we invite cognitive dissonance into our lives. We are conflicted by who we want to be and what the world around us says we should be. This can be recognised when we place too much value on whether everyone agrees with us and their opinion of us. We seek their approval as a means of moving forward and it limits us. It's an artificial ceiling that prevents us from moving on ideas at the right time.

Don't get me wrong, it is easily done – trust me, I know. In this world of real time feeds that display perfectly manicured "life" updates on social media that leave you feeling drained rather than rejuvenated. The bombardment of urgent notifications that mean you are required to respond asap, leading you into a state of constant overwhelm and a feeling of always being behind. Consuming social media and responding to outside noise that is programmed to keep you tuned in is a trap. It's like eating junk food and expecting to stay healthy. It's the thief of joy and a wolf in sheep's clothing. It promotes comparison, which steals joy and talks you out of trusting your gut, which is propagated by an underlying fear of not being good enough and a lack mindset. This is a dangerous cocktail to drink, especially for someone who is within striking distance of changing the full trajectory of their life and their family's life for generations to come. The required deep work has no chance to get a look in, unless you choose yourself.

I understand this is the way society and the workplace is structured right now, and it's hard to banish the seduction and

CHAPTER 12: SECURING YOUR FIRST DOMINO

gratification that comes from chasing external rewards. But the asymmetric upside of living in accordance with your inner values, purpose and bigger mission for your life and business is where real fulfilment is found. It has exponentiality baked into its very core that you must choose to prioritise this at all costs.

Fulfilment is what you are aiming for, but distraction and lack is likely what you've been force fed. Choose today to block it out, to be proud of the consistency of effort and chip away at the goal each day – this is progress, this is where the real gains are made. These are wins that we feel in our soul, the ones that matter. They help us to gain trust with ourselves, and this is where self-worth can skyrocket. By letting go of external validation and being hooked to the opinions of others, it releases us from being controlled in our daily mood and how we feel. This distraction is now gone.

By staying aligned with our true purpose and mission, our self-worth is attached to the right thing. There is such an incredible feeling that comes with achieving your inner goals.

Simon Sinek said it best, "Start measuring success based on the internal sense of purpose and growth you experience."

Choose to release the need for external validation, ignore it, unhook yourself from it and embrace the freedom that comes as a result. You will move differently when you don't get your sense of self-worth from other people's opinions, because then you are free to focus on what matters.

This is where you can be fully present with your clients and become a trusted advisor, because you are living in line with your values, and you trust yourself. This is where you become unstoppable because you can tap into the infinite possibility around you. You can engage with the ability to use your imagination to really create.

When you are proud of yourself, and your self-worth is derived from your ability to do the work, it's only boosted further when the work is to make connections everywhere you go, add value, give willingly, inspire others' growth and collaborate. It's magic! This is a life that's going to go places, that's doing big things and making a difference.

Know that your first domino is within reach and that you have infinite potential. There is a world where what you want already exists and now you are ready to step into it.

You have been changed by absorbing this book and each of the Domino Challenges was specifically crafted to create expansion. You are different now.

You recognise and respect yourself for leading with integrity, holding yourself accountable, being human and acknowledging the humanity in others. You have authentically shared your story and inspired others to move boldly, controlling your doubts, worries and fears and channeling your inner conversations towards abundance, possibility and growth.

EVERYTHING YOU NEED TO MAKE IT HAPPEN IS WITHIN YOU.

Think about what you've accomplished by finishing this book, and be proud of your transformation.

You've learned:

- How to reduce the friction and make it easier to attract the right clients to your business.
- How to plant good seeds that lead to huge outcomes.
- How to change your mental program and overcome your old excuses, fears and insecurities.
- How to trust your intuition and leverage it to your fullest advantage.
- How to create magic for yourself and for others at speed.

CHAPTER 12: SECURING YOUR FIRST DOMINO

- How to live an epic life that you love that brings you more clients and opportunity.
- How to ask questions at every stage of the conversation and exit with grace.
- How to adopt the winning mindset of an enthusiastic and energetic world-class salesperson and entrepreneur.
- How to rid energy drainers from your life and gain control over your emotional outbursts.
- How to illuminate the path for others by stepping boldly into the light.
- The power of sharing your story authentically and building trust and golden opportunities.
- How to organise and structure your day for magnetic sales success.
- How to uncover the real reason your client isn't moving forward and how to influence the close.
- How to trust yourself and the asymmetric upside and fulfillment that comes from living for your inner values and purpose.

That's a heck of a lot of "how to's" – you are a badass. Just think about what you've achieved in going through this process.

It's the simple but effective method of creating MAGIC that leads to landing your first domino.

Now you are ready to go out into the world and impart the following framework.

Make connections everywhere you go – speaking life into others' dreams.

Add value – by making valuable introductions and referrals, promoting others.

Give willingly – unattached to the outcome yet knowing that you are here to serve and it all comes back in unforeseen ways.

Inspire others' growth – through your own example and encouragement.

Collaborate – because that's where the real magic is found.

You are ready. The First Domino awaits. Be sure to let me know when it arrives (which will be soon if it hasn't already). I am celebrating your success every step of the way.

The First Domino is yours for the taking; it's already done. It is inevitable, now that is in the bag, so don't take your foot off the gas, don't get complacent and stop doing the process. The skill is to find ways to feed your hunger and amplify it. That is what all the greats do. You see this in sports with athletes like Kobe and Jordan, and in business with Musk and Bezos.

In any arena, those that perpetually win find ways to increase their hunger levels in the game they are playing. Jordan used to make up cutting insults from other players just to rile himself and lock in. Increase the MAGIC, amplify it and never get out of the rhythm. There's a lion in you waiting to be unleashed, and it all starts with one, one domino, one client, one win, one step, one thought, or one action. Now you're on your way, this is where you get to take it to fifty levels above, so never let that energy go.

CHAPTER 12: SECURING YOUR FIRST DOMINO

It's right when you are thinking about walking away that you are closest to a big breakthrough. Your only job is to find the win and not quit. Ultra-marathon runner and former Navy Seal, Chadd Wright says, "The harder it gets, the more I have to break it down." If you are struggling to make something work, chunk it down and just focus on a smaller component of the task in front of you. When asked how he's feeling during a 100-mile race and the pain is unbearable, he responds with "outstanding" every time. This is because he may not be able to change the outside circumstances (i.e. the race he has chosen to enter), but he can take control of the story he tells himself and how he responds.

Can I give you one more thing before we part ways?

You were born to do something special. You are here on purpose, reading this because it was written as destiny. That first client, that domino, is yours to win. It's all going to happen for you. Don't count yourself out, or put yourself down, or compare your journey to anyone else's. In life, people are so terribly bad at sales, so awful at client communication, team culture and empathy, that by putting into action the steps in this book you'll be miles ahead. Don't discount the value that you bring. You have something amazing to give your clients and the world.

You are not a shark, or an egomaniac, or a narcissist. You have so much going for you, but the world will have you believe that you are the crazy one for staying healthy, prioritising your personal development and your growth.

People may be jealous and threatened by your success. They may try to push their views on you, but stay fast and stay true. You are incredible, and there is only one of you – and that is your secret sauce! Give the world a gift by giving your full self to it. When you get in tune with your own rhythm and feel the soul of the world as the music to dance to, nothing and no one can stop what's planned.

THE FIRST DOMINO

A lot of why people struggle a whole lifetime can be overcome by taking a chance, living more in the unknown and pushing out of your comfort zone. We are only here for a short time, a blink of an eye, so why not go for it? This is where you accelerate and find a fuel that effortlessly magnetises your ability to land client after client. When you see problems as opportunities, you can be flexible and nimble and seek growth every day, and that is when you bulletproof your own success.

I want you to win. I want to hear about your "First Domino" stories. Please share them with me. Post a picture with your clients and the book, and please share this message with anyone who needs it. It's a movement and we help each other get better and improve. It's the small things we do that can have a big impact. I hope you find a place for this book in another person's life and give them the gift of fast tracking their business.

Big love,

Tim

PS. A portion of the profits from the sale of this book go to children with learning difficulties, ADHD and autism and families that have had their lives destroyed by flash floods and disasters.

A gift for you.

Just a reminder to download your free resources pack at **www.thefirstdominobook.com**. I've created these materials to accelerate your experience beyond the book.

Included is your 10 Domino Challenges Today Chart to print out and put up on your wall, the First Domino checklist, and 15 templates for LinkedIn posts and cold emails.

There's also a handy downloadable Big Buckets Tracker Template, which will allow you to feel in control and take

CHAPTER 12: SECURING YOUR FIRST DOMINO

ownership each week by visualising how you are progressing on each of your biggest needle-movers and big rocks.

Included on top of this is your Weekly Operating Principles Tracker - it's a reminder that you are on the right path. Week by week as you progress, you can pat yourself on the back for raising the standard.

I get it: there can be a sense of overwhelm and, when needing to change behaviours, it can be easy to lose track of the gains you make. This causes people to quit. With this visual representation of your progress, you can cross out each day as you go. It will help you to stay motivated and avoid being hard on yourself because you've achieved your goal and you can see that you are going in the right direction.

If you are at a particular point of stress in your work, this will give you a sense of control, to be able to track things. People drop out when they lose a sense of control. Install these behaviours for the next 90 days and make them the best you've ever lived.

- Go to bed at 9-9.30pm every night, get up at 4.30-5am every morning.
- Exercise daily and make it a part of your identity.
- Read 10-20 pages per day.
- Write down new ideas as they appear in the moment.
- Note down all you have to be grateful for in your phone.
- Review your goals 3-5 times a day.
- Live as if your goal has already happened in attitude, mind and feeling.
- Remember, it's about who you become in the process.
- The lifestyle you create is the real gold.

SOURCES

en.wikipedia.org/wiki/Michael_Phelps

www.sportskeeda.com/us/olympics/michael-phelps-opened-missing-single-day-training-five-years

paulgraham.com/ds.html

www.linkedin.com/posts/neilkpatel_youre-sending-emails-during-the-wrong-day-activity-7266229035163111424-CcZT/

www.youtube.com/watch?v=HqrEr7MMSew

x.com/timjcarden

BOOKS THAT INSPIRED ME

Optimism and energy

The Energy Bus by Jon Gordon
Greenlights by Matthew McConaughey

Mindset

The Power of Your Subconscious Mind by Joseph Murphy

Quantum leaps

you² by Price Pritchett

Taking action

Living With A Seal by Jesse Itzler

Persistence

The Alchemist by Paulo Coelho

THE FIRST DOMINO

The Greatest Salesman In The World by Og Mandino

Podcast episodes
worth listening to

The Tim Castle Show – John McMahon – The Qualifed Sales Leader **podcasts.apple.com/sg/podcast/the-qualified-sales-leader-mastering-meddpicc-how-to/id1522135380?i=1000659137136**

John Kaplan – *Force Management* podcast **soundcloud.com/force-management-1/how-to-trap-your-competition**
Chad Wright – *The Resilient Show* **podcasts.apple.com/ca/podcast/chadd-wright-mental-toughness-faith-lessons-from-a/id1695040954?i=1000680547753**

The Tim Castle Show – Matt Dixon – The Jolt Effect
www.youtube.com/watch?v=wSBlgAxnE5A

You can contact me on **tim@timjscastle.com**. Hit me up.

Follow me on @timjscastle on social. Tag the book and your wins.

Website: Visit **www.timjscastle.com** for more of Tim's wisdom, tools and resources to help you elevate your success in negotiation, sales and mindset. Find out more about Tim's work at the intersection of AI and negotiation helping you maximise influence, persuasion and value creation in an AI centric world at **www.thenegotiatorsedge.ai**. Feel free to contact us for speaking, training, and workshops.

My podcast is *The Tim Castle Show*. This is where I meet courageous people doing inspirational things around the world. We've had elite athletes like James Lawrence, Iron Cowboy, best-selling authors like Chris Jarvis and high-performance coaches like Annalie Howling. Topics include self-worth, endurance, mindset, mountain climbing, record breaking, attachment styles, business, entrepreneurship, sales and negotiation and much more. You're going to love it!

BE THE LION

How to Overcome Big Challenges and Make It Happen

WANT TO ACHIEVE MORE WITHOUT THE STRESS AND OVERWHELM?

As an ambitious person, I inevitably have a lot on my plate. In just two years, I went through pretty much every life change you can imagine. I planned our wedding, got married, moved jobs, moved countries, wrote and published a book, completed an MBA, became a father to my baby son and then coped with his sudden serious illness, all whilst working full time.

I had to be the lion. I created new habits and thought

patterns and reconnected with my purpose to get shit done. I became stronger, a master of time management, productivity and motivation. As a result, my goals got closer. And there was a surprising side-effect: I became happier and more relaxed.

LET ME SHOW YOU HOW TO SET THE BAR HIGH AND SUCCEED.

I distilled everything I learned into my 4Cs model, which enables you to overcome any challenge.

This book explains the 4Cs and teaches processes, strategies and optimisations to turbocharge your life. This system will help you to achieve more, without any of the stress, overwhelm and fear that often comes with big life changes. Taking yourself to the next level and achieving huge success should be joyful. So, let's have some fun...

PRAISE

"I want to talk about my friend here, Tim Castle, and his amazing book *Be the Lion*.

"I don't have a whole lot of time to read, but when I do, I want to read really, really good things, and this book is something that everybody should check out. 1. *Be The Lion* is an awesome title; 2. It's an awesome cover; 3. He goes through a really cool process that outlines his 4Cs for how to get through really, really big challenges and difficult situations. There's a lot to go through. I mean, he really, really knows his stuff, but take it from me: you need to check out this book right now and find the Lion within you!"

- **Ryan Serhant,**
Sell It Like Serhant, Million Dollar Listing New York,
SERHANT.

THE MOMENTUM SALES MODEL

How to achieve success in sales, exceed targets and generate explosive growth

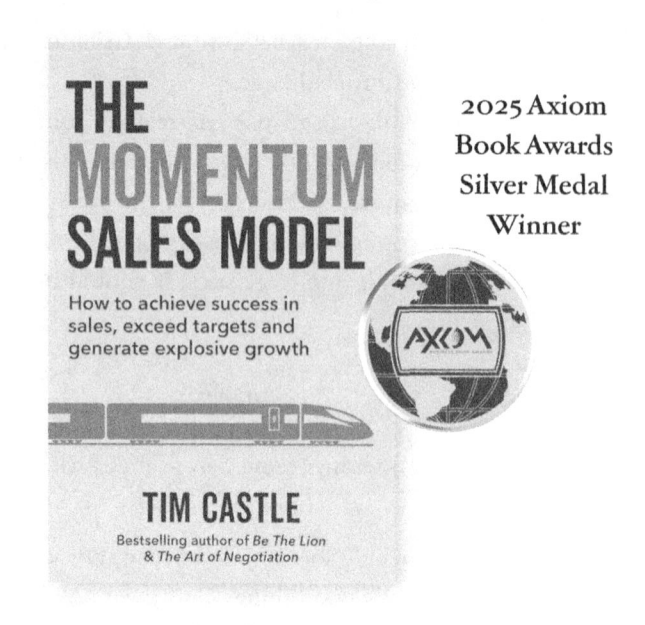

2025 Axiom Book Awards Silver Medal Winner

PRAISE

Hustle Inspires Hustle – Best Sales Books for Experts

"Tim Castle's *The Momentum Sales Model* offers a fresh perspective on building and maintaining sales momentum. The book emphasises creating a systematic approach to sales that focuses on consistency and continuous improvement.

"Castle's model helps salespeople develop habits and strategies that drive sustained success, making it a valuable resource for those looking to enhance their sales processes."

Book Life Prize 2023 - Quarter Finalist

Plot/Idea: 9 out of 10
Originality: 9 out of 10
Prose: 9 out of 10
Character/Execution: 10 out of 10
Overall: 9.25 out of 10

Assessment:

Plot/Idea: Castle offers readers functional sales strategies aimed at producing a financially stable business model. The advice is geared towards building future business success as well, using Castle's distinctive Momentum Sales Model as the basis for sales growth.

Originality: This is a well-rounded, user-friendly guide that pulls from real life examples. The book's structure adds to its originality, as Castle provides readers his uniquely developed sales model paired with a myriad of engaging ideas.

Prose: The prose is convincing and eloquent; Castle writes in an easy-to-follow style that makes the information understandable and charismatic.

Character/Execution: Castle offers hands-on examples throughout, combined with down-to-earth guidance that readers will find easy to understand and apply. He includes several visuals as well that add to the guide's appeal.

Business Book Awards 2024 Finalist - Sales & Marketing

THE ART OF NEGOTIATION

How to get what you want (every time)

International Bestseller in multiple countries. #1 in Job Interviews on Amazon, consistently Top 10 in the negotiation category on Amazon. If you're looking to improve your everyday negotiations this book can help.

MORE FROM TIM CASTLE

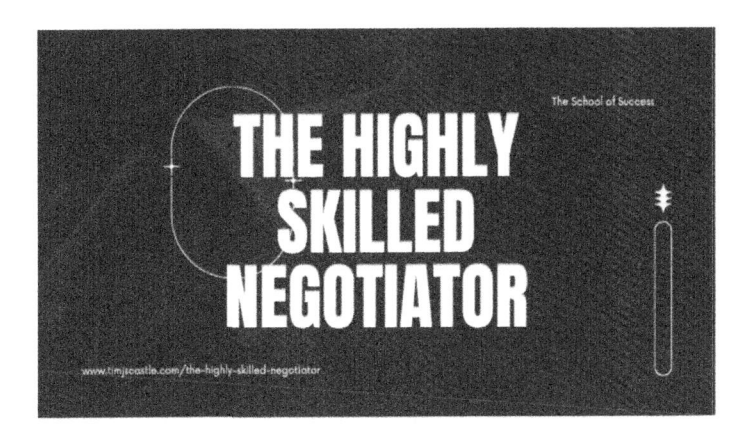

THE HIGHLY SKILLED NEGOTIATOR

The School of Success

www.timjscastle.com/the-highly-skilled-negotiator

This online training is designed to enhance negotiation skills for both personal and professional success.

Covering over **80 lessons**, it teaches communication, persuasion, influence, language, confidence, strategies for overcoming objections and closing deals.

Enrolment also includes a *free bonus* course on the vital topic of **Job Interview Mastery**.

Negotiation is the number 1 high leverage skill today!

ENROL NOW

https://www.timjscastle.com/the-highly-skilled-negotiator

YOU GOT THIS

NOW GO CREATE SOME MAGIC!